SUSIE CROSBY

JUST ONE WORD

HARVEST HOUSE PUBLISHERS
EUGENE, OREGON

Unless otherwise indicated, all Scripture quotations are taken from THE MESSAGE, copyright © 1993, 1994, 1995, 1996, 2000, 2001, 2002 by Eugene H. Peterson. Used by permission of NavPress. All rights reserved. Represented by Tyndale House Publishers, Inc.

Verses marked NIV are taken from the Holy Bible, New International Version®, NIV®. Copyright © 1973, 1978, 1984, 2011 by Biblica, Inc.® Used by permission. All rights reserved worldwide.

Verses marked NASB are taken from the New American Standard Bible®, © 1960, 1962, 1963, 1968, 1971, 1972, 1973, 1975, 1977, 1995 by The Lockman Foundation. Used by permission. (www.Lockman.org)

Definition sources used in this book are distinguished in Notes.

Cover design and illustration by Emily Weigel Design

Backcover Author photo by Life N Light

Just One Word

Copyright © 2018 Susie Crosby
Published by Harvest House Publishers
Eugene, Oregon 97408
www.harvesthousepublishers.com

ISBN 978-0-7369-7480-6 (pbk.)
ISBN 978-0-7369-7481-3 (eBook)

Library of Congress Cataloging-in-Publication Data
Names: Crosby, Susie, author.
Title: Just one word / Susie Crosby.
Description: Eugene, Oregon : Harvest House Publishers, [2018]
Identifiers: LCCN 2018000637 (print) | LCCN 2018022911 (ebook) | ISBN 9780736974813 (ebook) | ISBN 9780736974806 (pbk.)
Subjects: LCSH: Meditations.
Classification: LCC BV4832.3 (ebook) | LCC BV4832.3 .C76 2018 (print) | DDC 242/.2--dc23
LC record available at https://lccn.loc.gov/2018000637

Printed in the United States of America

18 19 20 21 22 23 24 25 26 / Bang-GL / 10 9 8 7 6 5 4 3 2 1

CONTENTS

For Mom
Thank you for loving words, people, and Jesus
and for teaching us to love them too.
You are such a special part of this.

Say only what helps, each word a gift.
EPHESIANS 4:29

Part One

God's Peace

DISPLACE

verb: to move physically out of position; to take the place of

*It's wonderful what happens when Christ
displaces worry at the center of your life.*
PHILIPPIANS 4:7

Are you a worrier? I am. I hate to admit it, but I really am. My first thought when I wake up in the morning is often something stressful.

What if...?
I don't know what to do about...
How am I going to...?
This is too hard...

The center of our lives. Our hearts, our souls, our minds. Worry and fear are not supposed to have that place.

Christ wants to be there. He wants to calm us, heal us, hold us through the stresses and struggles. He can *displace* our worries.

Displace means "to move physically out of position; to take the place of." That's what boats do to water. A huge tanker stacked with freight, a ferry loaded with hundreds of cars, a weathered old rowboat. The mass of the boat pushes the water out of the way and literally takes its place.

So the displaced worries? They're floating around somewhere. Of course we are going to think about the things in our life that concern us. But if we let Jesus be our lifeboat of peace, if we focus on him, those anxious thoughts get smaller as they drift further away from our hearts.

Invite Him In

Take a deep breath. Think for a minute about your heart, your soul, your mind. What is taking up the center of you today? If it's not Jesus, ask him to move things around. He can displace the fear, anxiety, and negativity and fill you with his peace, deep joy, and real hope. Allow the worry to float away from you and hold on to him. He knows what you need.

Prayer

Dear Jesus, thank you that you care deeply about what concerns me. You know the weight of my stress, and you are willing to get in the middle of it all. Please let your strength and love and peace *displace* my worries and calm my heart.

UNFOLDING

verb: revealing, making clear by gradual disclosure

*Even though on the outside it often looks like things are
falling apart on us, on the inside, where God is making
new life, not a day goes by without his unfolding grace.*
2 CORINTHIANS 4:16

Fear. We all experience it. We are afraid of things real and imagined, now and in the future. We worry a lot about what is ahead, the unpredictable—especially when we don't know what it is.

So we try all kinds of ways to figure out what's going to happen, what to expect. When I was in elementary school, my friends and I made "fortune tellers" out of notebook paper. We would put our thumbs and index fingers inside the carefully folded triangles of paper and ask each other to choose a color, number, or word that we had written on the inside parts. We'd open and close the little contraption a few times and then lift a flap to reveal something significant, like who we were going to marry or how many children we were going to have.

We loved this silly game. But isn't it interesting that even at eight years old, we were trying to predict our futures? We were looking for some indication of what was going to happen in our lives. We wanted to know how it all was going to end up. We wanted to know everything right then.

But God doesn't give us everything at once. He lovingly protects us from knowing too much in advance. When it comes to letting us in on his plans for us, he does something fascinating and frustrating at the same time.

He unfolds.

He opens up to us just enough knowledge, just enough strength, just enough of him for each day. *Gradual* disclosure. Sometimes slower than we would like and less than we might want. But exactly what we need.

Jesus knows what he is doing. He lifts a flap for us, gives us a peek. Shows us the next turn, but not the whole journey. Gives us a direction, but not the destination. Most of the time, we just have to trust him for all the yet-to-be revealed parts of our lives. And know that he is right there with us every step of the way.

INVITE HIM IN

Look for God's unfolding beauty and grace as you strive to follow him. Thank him for what he is revealing to you and try to trust him for what he hasn't yet shown you. He's not playing games: He holds your future, and more importantly, he holds *you*. Let him steady you and fill you with peace as he opens up your life a little bit more today.

PRAYER

Dear Jesus, thank you for the way you reveal your grace. You are always making things new—including me. I will trust in your goodness, your love, and your perfect timing as you *unfold* your plans for my life.

Instead

adverb: as an alternative or substitute for; in place of, rather

*Instead of worrying, pray. Let petitions and praises shape
your worries into prayers, letting God know your concerns.
Before you know it, a sense of God's wholeness, everything
coming together for good, will come and settle you down.*
PHILIPPIANS 4:6-7

Decisions are hard for most people. I learned this working in an ice cream shop during high school and college. Baskin-Robbins, also known as "31 Flavors," was a popular place. Those of us who worked there knew that there were actually more than 31 flavors most of the time. The ice cream cases held 48 different tubs, and there were even more back in the freezer.

It was difficult for people to choose. Go with the favorite, or try the new flavor of the month? In a chocolaty mood, or did a fruit flavor sound better? For the little ones, it was really a struggle. Bubblegum or rainbow sherbet? Or maybe just plain vanilla instead?

The word *instead* usually implies a choice, a decision. So when Paul tells us, "Instead of worrying, pray," the next step is up to us. To pray instead of worrying is a choice. It is a discipline that doesn't come easily.

Pray *as an alternative* to worrying.

Substitute prayer for worry.

Rather than worrying, pray.

We try to do this, but we usually end up doing a little of both. We pray *and* worry. But that doesn't bring the peace, the sense of wholeness that Jesus wants to give us. He wants us to trust him completely.

To make the decision to pray *in place of* worrying. To thank him and praise him even before we see his answers.

He waits for us to just order the ice cream already. He wants us to decide, believing that he can handle it and that he really is working all things together for good (Romans 8:28).

> The root choice is to trust at all times that God is with you and will give you what you most need...God says to you, "I love you, I am with you..." This is the voice to listen to. And that listening requires a real choice.[1]

Invite Him In

Try it. Ask God to help you choose to pray instead of worrying about something today. He will help you put your requests, your needs in his hands—and leave them there. Let him assure you that everything is coming together for good. Then, take a deep breath of peace as his wholeness envelops you and settles you down. You can trust him completely.

Prayer

Dear Jesus, thank you that I can bring everything to you. Please help me choose to trust you with all my stress. You are the only one who can take my fearful concerns and give me your peace *instead*.

Outcome

noun: something that follows as a consequence; a result

*Christ's death was also a one-time event, but it was a sacrifice
that took care of sins forever. And so, when he next appears,
the outcome for those eager to greet him is, precisely, salvation.*
HEBREWS 9:28

My husband and I love sports, especially football and baseball. We enjoy getting caught up in the energy of the crowd, the competitive spirit. And the most exciting part? I think it's the unpredictability, the suspense, the fact that no one ever knows ahead of time who is going to win the game.

But we don't really like that unpredictability when it comes to real life, do we? We want to know how things are going to turn out. We don't like to wonder about or wait for the outcome.

When I write in my prayer journal, I start by thanking God for so many things. But it doesn't take long for my thanks to turn into requests, and my requests to spin into worries.

- *How is this ever going to work out?*
- *What if the test results aren't good? What if healing doesn't come?*
- *Where are you, God? Are you going to come through? And may I ask—when?*

We want to predict. We want to be sure. We want to know the outcome, but we don't always get to. Jesus is the only one who does. And here is what he tells us in Revelation 21:4-5: "He'll wipe every tear from their eyes. Death is gone for good—tears gone, crying gone, pain gone—all the first order of things gone…Look! I'm making everything new."

The hard stuff of this life is just hard. It's messy; it's unpredictable; and we lose sometimes. We don't always get the outcome we are hoping for. He doesn't promise that. What he does promise is to be with us through it all, to bring his grace and peace to everything we ask him to.

Because of his sacrifice for us, we have so much hope. We have his absolute assurance, his promises of victory and healing, freedom and peace, redemption and joy. The final outcome for those of us who belong to him? "Precisely, salvation."

How amazing we get to know ahead of time that we are going to win!

INVITE HIM IN

Place your worries before God and let him hold your fears and future. Ask him to help you trust him as you relinquish your grip of control to him. No matter what you are facing, the final outcome is in his hands. And so are you.

PRAYER

Dear Jesus, thank you that your sacrifice took care of all my worry, all my sin, and all my sorrow. I look forward with confidence to the final redemption and the victory of your return. No matter what I face in this life, my *outcome* will be overwhelming joy and peace with you in heaven forever.

REST

noun: breathing space, downtime, peace of mind or spirit

Are you tired? Worn out? Burned out on religion?
Come to me. Get away with me and you'll recover
your life. I'll show you how to take a real rest.
Matthew 11:28

A "real rest"? What does that even mean?

I'm pretty sure Jesus has more in mind for us than a short nap or a day off. As good as those sound, I'm curious about this idea of *real* rest. Because what I feel a lot of the time is rest*less*. Even on vacation. I'm writing this in the middle of summer break. And I actually have taken a nap this week. Yet I'm unsettled, fidgety, antsy.

I have way too many things on my list.

I'm worrying about so many things, so many people.

I'm not doing enough.

I should, I should, I should...

"Jesus, what do *you* want me to do?"

And he is quiet. So I squirm and wriggle and try to run ahead. Then I read this: "Come to me. Get away with me and you'll recover your life."

"But how, Jesus? We're kind of burning out here. How do we recover our lives? How do we rest in you? You understand that we have to go to work and school, run our errands, take care of laundry and homework and bills, right? Most of the things on our everyday lists are not optional. Are you telling us not to do them? To just run away from it all?"

Then I read the next verse: "Walk with me and work with me—watch how I do it" (Matthew 11:29).

Oh. Maybe what Jesus means by *rest* is *a deep breath in the midst of it all*. In the stress of our busy schedules and sleepless nights and multitasking, we can come to Jesus. He will walk alongside us and be right there with us as we try to get everything done. As we hustle and worry, he reminds us to look to him. He wants to give us a break as we let him hold everything for a minute, or a night, or the rest of our lives.

INVITE HIM IN

Are you restless? Jesus can help you. He will weave meaning and hope through everything that is happening in your world. Just for a moment, can you stop and take a long, deep breath? Maybe another one? *He is God.* Be still. Know that. Trust him. Look to him when everything is churning inside you. Ask him to calm your restless heart. He is the only one who can give you lasting peace, abundant life, and real rest.

PRAYER

Dear Jesus, I want to know what it feels like to live my life with your Spirit setting the pace. Every moment, I need you to walk and work right beside me. Thank you for showing me how to recover my life and find real *rest* in you.

HOLD

verb: to grasp, carry, or support with one's arms or hands

I hold on to you for dear life, and you hold me.
PSALM 63:8

We hold on to God, and he holds on to us. At the same time. In different ways.

When we hold on to God, we cling to him. We believe in his truth; we trust his promises; we look to him for help. We squeeze his hand tight to make sure he is there. We are the weaker ones, holding on with all we've got.

And as the stronger one, God holds on to us. He supports us. He keeps us close. He establishes us and helps us stand. No matter what is swirling around us, he keeps us steady. We are completely secure in his hands.

The other day, I saw a dad walking his little girl through the parking lot to the grocery store. She was little, probably two or three, and he looked like a linebacker. Her tiny hand disappeared in his as she reached up and he reached down, both holding on to each other.

She was safe; he was sure. Even if she lost her footing, he would keep her from falling to the ground. Even if she tried to wriggle away, he would not let her go. She was never in danger, despite the drivers all around them who were backing up, rushing in and out of the lot, distracted.

She was safe because she was holding on to him.

And she was even safer because she was held by him.

We are too. Our heavenly Father reaches down and takes our little hands as we walk through this scary world. Whether the dangers and fears are real, imagined, or something we aren't even aware of, he knows. "Don't panic," he says. "I'm with you. There's no need to fear for I'm your God. I'll give you strength. I'll help you. I'll hold you steady, keep a firm grip on you" (Isaiah 41:10).

We are safe when we hold on to him.

And we are even safer when we are held by him.

INVITE HIM IN

Reach up to Jesus. Let him take your hand and hold you close. He is your good Father, your strong protector. He is reaching down to guide you through the stress and strain of your life. Even if you feel scared, even if you miss a step, even if you try to wriggle away...he's got you. And he won't let you go.

PRAYER

Dear Jesus, thank you that you *hold* me close and keep me safe. I reach for your hand and cling to you as tightly as I can. Help me trust you and believe that even when my hand is slipping, yours is strong and sure.

RUN

verb: to move freely about at will, to go without restraint

Because you've always stood up for me, I'm free to run and play.
Psalm 63:7

Doesn't that sound fun? To just be free to run and play?

Kids do it all the time. When a classroom door opens for recess, the little ones practically explode out of there. And most of them don't stop when they get to the playground. They start playing tag or soccer, sprinting and scurrying from the tetherball game to the swings to the monkey bars.

It makes me smile.

Most of us have forgotten how good it feels to simply run and play. Not the kind of running where we plod along the track or treadmill to burn calories, but the kind that we just can't keep from doing. Of course, our bodies aren't as bouncy or our energy levels as high as when we were six years old, but the little kid inside us still longs for that freedom.

David wrote Psalm 63 when he was being pursued by his enemies, struggling and hiding in the rough and barren Judean desert. Needless to say, it was not a very good time in his life. Yet, even here he was able to experience childlike exuberance and joy because he knew *for sure* that God had his back.

What about us? A lot of the time, we are in rough places too. Maybe we are experiencing a lonely time, a confusing situation, or a season of fear. These can last a lot longer than we would like. But we don't have to wait for them to be over to have a little fun, to take a little break. We can run and play because God is standing up for us. Always. He is watching over us, holding on to us, working in and around us—even in the worst of times.

So can we let ourselves escape for a few minutes? Can we run to the playground in our hearts? I bet it would make Jesus smile too.

INVITE HIM IN

Run to him. He will take you in his arms and swing you around and let you know that you are safe. He is watching out for you, and you can relax in his protective care. Go ahead and play for a bit. Swing, climb, jump, run...and thank him for standing up for you. You are free in his love today. Enjoy your recess!

PRAYER

Dear Jesus, you are my helper, and you take such good care of me! Thank you for providing a safe place where I can escape from the pressures and expectations that confine me. You fill me with joy as I *run* to you.

WRECK

noun: the broken remains of something ruined; a
person of broken constitution, health, or spirits

All my insides are on fire,
my body is a wreck.
I'm on my last legs; I've had it.
PSALM 38:7-8

"She's a wreck."

"He's just wrecked."

I imagine a car after a terrible accident. Smashed metal, broken glass, turned the wrong way or upside down, wheels bent, tires flat, and steam coming out everywhere.

Have you ever described someone that way? Something must be really wrong for us to use that word. Someone we know must be experiencing an awful time. Their physical or emotional strength is failing. They are crushed, broken, unable to function.

We will probably all feel like this at some point. Many things in this life can damage our bodies and our spirits. The things we hope and pray for—the job, the relationship, the acceptance letter, the healing—don't happen. The things we don't expect—disease, rejection, loss, accidents, divorce, abuse—sometimes do.

The painful things in this life can wreck us to our core.

Jesus knows this pain. He was accused and taunted, violently beaten, and nailed to a cross to die. His pain was crushingly physical and deeply emotional, but most of all, it was spiritual. What really wrecked Jesus as he suffered through this brutal sacrifice was being separated from God. Feeling forsaken by his Father, his closest relationship, his whole world...It must have been excruciating.

Because of what he did on that cross, things are different for us. No matter what is happening in our lives, we don't ever have to be completely wrecked in our souls. We don't have to be without our God for one single second. In the times of feeling mentally or physically destroyed, we are still held by him, closer than ever. Because of his love for us, we will never have to endure the agony of being separated from the open arms of our Father, our closest friend. As Romans 8:39 promises, "Absolutely nothing can get between us and God's love."

INVITE HIM IN

When you feel like you've got nothing left, remember that you still have Jesus. Always. Absolutely nothing can separate you two. He won't let anything wreck you completely. Bring to him the anger, fear, shakiness, questions, pain. He is right there to calm you and restore you physically, emotionally, and spiritually. Let him hold you close.

PRAYER

Dear Jesus, only you can soothe my weary soul. When I feel like a *wreck*, I will quietly wait for you to come and rescue me. Thank you that no matter how broken I am, you can restore me and bring me back to wholeness in you.

Prepared

adjective: ready or able to deal with
something, equipped, all set

*Be prepared. You're up against far more than you can handle on your
own. Take all the help you can get, every weapon God has issued.*
EPHESIANS 6:13

Hurricanes, earthquakes, floods, wildfires...natural disasters are devastating. Imagining such a disaster happening in my little part of
the world scares me to death. I tend to go into "it won't really happen here" mode. Maybe if I just don't think about it...

But at the school where I teach, I have to think about it. We have
practice drills every month.

For our first big one in the fall, the email to staff reads, "Earth-
quake drill. Get ready."

Ready? I was not. Even after reading the detailed directions, I
felt nervous and unprepared. At the last minute, I grabbed a Post-
it note and wrote a few key things to remember. I felt better once I
had my "cheat sheet."

Being prepared. "Ready or able to deal with something." The
preparation is always worth it, because emergencies happen when
we least expect them.

And so do spiritual attacks. Crises of faith come out of the blue.
We usually are just going along with our daily lives, trying to live for
Jesus, when the enemy sneaks up on us. He deceives us. All of a sud-
den, we are in a battle we didn't anticipate.

Doubt, fear, guilt, and discouragement make us feel far from
God, causing us to wonder if he is really there. Everything seems

dark, unsettled, scary, confusing. We know God's truth, but we panic as we try to remember.

Maybe we need a "cheat sheet" for times like these.

Doubting if God really cares about you? "God not only loves you very much but also has put his hand on you for something special" (1 Thessalonians 1:4).

Feeling like he isn't listening? "If you make yourselves at home with me and my words are at home in you, you can be sure that whatever you ask will be listened to and acted upon" (John 15:7).

Wondering if you can be forgiven? "Count yourself lucky, how happy you must be—you get a fresh start, your slate's wiped clean...God holds nothing against you and you're holding nothing back from him" (Psalm 32:1-2).

Afraid of the future? "GOD is striding ahead of you. He's right there with you. He won't let you down; he won't leave you. Don't be intimidated. Don't worry" (Deuteronomy 31:8).

INVITE HIM IN

Jesus can prepare your heart with the truth of his words. He will give you his presence, his answers, his victory in these battles. For the ultimate "cheat sheet," just call on his name. Everything you need can be found in the precious and powerful name of Jesus.

PRAYER

Dear Jesus, thank you that you have given me your words to protect and *prepare* me. Please help me remember them always and make me ready for the battles ahead.

NEWS

noun: previously unknown information, a report
of recent events, an announcement

*It's news I'm most proud to proclaim, this extraordinary Message
of God's powerful plan to rescue everyone who trusts him.*
Romans 1:16

What is going on?

We want to know; we need to know. News of what is happening in our communities, our countries, our world is so important. There are lots of reasons why we should pay attention to the news.

And it's not hard to find. We hear it; we watch it; we get updates on our phones. What's interesting to me is that no matter where we get our information, we call it "the news." *The* news. Sometimes we call it local news, world news, good news, bad news, old news, or breaking news, but we refer to all kinds when we talk about "the news."

"Did you hear *the news*?"

"Are you watching *the news*?"

"It might be on *the news*."

Like it is the only "news" there is.

No matter how devastating, shocking, maddening, or frighteningly close to us today's stories are, they are *not* the only news. There is news breaking every day that we need to tune in to. It is the good news—the *best* news—of Jesus's love and redemption. It is the life-changing message that God wants everyone to hear and respond to.

It is his message of freedom and forgiveness and hope. It's his message that what we see, what we hear right now, is not the end of

27

the story. There is a bigger story going on with a much happier ending ahead. I wish this could tick across the bottom of every television screen, headline every article, and pop up on our phones each day.

When the daily or nightly news is tragic, scary, and disheartening, what will we do? Will we take action to help people, to change things for the better, to pray? Will we remember that it is not the *only* news? Will we be open to sharing the best news ever with all people in every corner of the earth?

Let's be proud to proclaim the love of Jesus. It's really good news.

INVITE HIM IN

Turn to Jesus for a reminder of his good news today. No matter what is going on in the world, your community, your home, or your heart, his powerful message of redemption endures. Let him show you what is true and remind you of the hope he brings. Every morning. Every evening. Every hour of every day. His powerful plan to rescue us, his incredible love that triumphs over evil—that's our top story.

PRAYER

Dear Jesus, your gospel—your true story—is refreshing, encouraging, and transforming. Thank you for the hope that comes from your powerful message of salvation. Please lead me to share this good *news* that comes from you today.

Part Two

God's Protection

FIERCE

adjective: showing a heartfelt and powerful
intensity; aggressive, forceful

GOD, a most fierce warrior, is at my side.
JEREMIAH 20:11

The word *fierce* brings to mind snarling teeth, menacing eyes, and unbridled anger. The thought of a wild animal or person being fierce toward us is terrifying.

Thinking about our loving, caring God as fierce is conflicting. We don't want to be scared of him. As powerful and wild and wise as he is, it scares us to think of him as fierce.

Unless he is being fierce *for* us...because we really need him to be. We all need a strong warrior on our side.

Life can be such a battle. Mentally, we fight negative self-talk, constant worrying, and overthinking every decision. Physically, we struggle with our bodies, food, exercise, sickness, pain, and fatigue. Emotionally, we are overcome with grief, anger, depression, anxiety, and loneliness. Spiritually, we feel defeated; we sin (again and again); we doubt God; we give in to temptation.

Whether we realize it or not, we are fighting an evil enemy. An enemy who looks for ways to hurt us, deceive us, destroy us, and keep us from trusting Jesus.

We fight these battles constantly. And Jesus knows them all. From the everyday choices we face to the overarching spiritual battle for our souls, he stands with us, reassuring us that he has already won. He has defeated the enemy of this world, and he wants us to rise victorious with him.

God is fierce *toward* sin; he is fierce *for* us. His heartfelt intensity works in our favor. He is aggressive and forceful in the way he fights for us. We matter immensely to him. We are his precious people.

And he is our "most fierce warrior." He is at our side.

INVITE HIM IN

Let him stand right beside you. Let him be your bodyguard, your protector as you fight today. Whatever you are facing, ask him to help you win the battle. He will. He wants you to overcome. He will protect you—fiercely.

PRAYER

Dear Jesus, thank you that your *fierce* love protects me constantly. Help me to know the strength of your presence. I want to live in the assurance that nothing can defeat me when you are by my side.

STRENGTH

noun: the emotional or mental qualities necessary in dealing
with distressing or difficult situations; toughness, resilience, grit

My grace is enough; it's all you need.
My strength comes into its own in your weakness.
2 CORINTHIANS 12:9

Do you feel strong? If you are like me, I would bet that most of the time you don't.

Strength makes me think of people with well-defined muscles, influential personalities, amazing stamina, and resilient hearts. All of these impress me. None of them come easily.

Most of us struggle for strength in many important aspects of our lives: eating habits, organization, communication, exercise, finances, handling our emotions, growing spiritually...the list is long.

So when we feel weak, when we are not doing very well, are we just supposed to keep trying harder and harder? Is that how we are supposed to gain strength? Answer the emails, go to the gym, clean out a couple of closets, make a healthy dinner, start a new Bible study, plow through the pile of bills. Stay up later, get up earlier, try not to cry as we just keep going.

We do this. We work harder and faster, but we don't get any stronger. Usually, after this kind of trying, we end up weaker and more depleted than before. Feelings of failure and discouragement reinforce our fears that we can't do enough or be enough, that we really don't have the strength we were hoping for after all.

But this cycle does not need to keep repeating itself. It can be different for those of us who know Jesus.

He is our source of strength—"the One who is strong enough to make [us] strong" (Romans 16:25).

His strength. That's what we really need. When we trust him with the hardest things, with the weaknesses that we are so ashamed of, his power can be revealed. When we ask him to give us *his* strength, he will. He won't necessarily take away our weaknesses, but he will work mightily in and through us. He will surprise us with the strength of his gentle grace. In our weakness, he is strong.

INVITE HIM IN

Look to Jesus. He wants to strengthen you, to make you solid and powerful in things that really matter, and he will. Just ask him. You don't have to work so hard; you don't have to muster up all that determination and energy on your own. Bring him your strengths *and* your weaknesses. You will be amazed at how much good he can do with both.

PRAYER

Dear Jesus, your overwhelming grace and *strength* are revealed in my weakness. Thank you that when I don't feel like enough, you are. Please remind me in my weakest times to lean into you and find everything I need.

NAKED

adjective: without the usual covering or protection; undisguised

I was afraid because I was naked. And I hid.
GENESIS 3:10

That dream you have sometimes about being naked in public? You know, the one where you wake up and laugh (or cry) in relief that it wasn't real? We've all had them. And we all fear it—the most private parts of our bodies being exposed for all to see. Something about nakedness makes us feel, well, lots of things: awkward, unprotected, vulnerable, ashamed, raw.

Whew. Tough words. Tougher emotions.

What about when you are fully clothed, but you *feel* naked? When your insides start to show, and you are desperately trying to keep them under wraps?

Please don't let anyone see...

...that my heart races when I think I might be disappointing someone.

...that I struggle with unrealistic expectations of "perfect," "favorite," and "best."

...that even though I'm all grown up, I cry because I miss my mom.

...that wrapped up in my nice, helpful, giving ways is a desperate need for approval.

...that sometimes, I'm just plain scared to death.

Isn't it exhausting to pretend we have it all together? Maybe it would be a relief to come out of hiding and begin to let our true selves be known. Maybe because of what Jesus thinks of us, we don't have to worry so much about protecting our hearts from what other people think. Maybe what really matters is being true to who he made us.

What if accepting our flaws and failures could reveal to us more about our strengths and gifts?

What if allowing ourselves to be vulnerable could connect us to our people in refreshing and meaningful ways?

What if we dared to show ourselves *undisguised*?

INVITE HIM IN

Can you trust Jesus with who you are? He made you. He knows exactly how you are wired, and he delights in every detail of you. He wants you to experience the depth of love and joy that comes from being known for who you really are. You can take off your usual covering just a little bit at a time...or all at once. Will it hurt? Maybe. Will you find life more abundant, more fulfilling, more real? Absolutely. He's got you covered.

PRAYER

Dear Jesus, thank you that I don't have to be afraid or embarrassed when my true self is *naked* before you. You know everything about me, and you love me more than I can even imagine. Please help me trust you enough to uncover my heart.

PATH

noun: way of life, conduct, or thought; route or course

*May the Master take you by the hand and lead you along
the path of God's love and Christ's endurance.*
2 Thessalonians 3:5

In the Pacific Northwest, we love to hike. It's exhilarating. We hike trails that lead through old forests, along rivers, or through alpine meadows bursting with wildflowers. We hike to lakes, beaches, lookouts, or mountaintops. The views are magnificent.

Hiking can be relaxing and fun or challenging and exhausting. The important thing is to stay on the designated trails, though. It would be dangerous to try to reach the end of the hike without following the path designed for hikers.

It's the same when we follow God. We want to experience the reward, the destination of heaven with him at the end of our lives. But we need to stay on the right path.

I used to be so scared about this. I thought this path he had made for me was so narrow, so rigid that if I took a wrong turn, I would be lost forever. If I went the wrong way, I wouldn't get to go any further. Still, the path sometimes seemed confining and restrictive...and I accidentally (or maybe on purpose) wandered off. Several times.

And here's what I discovered as I tripped and struggled along the unstable ground and slippery places:

The path of God's love is beautiful, with unimaginable surprises around every corner. He walks with us every step of the way, delighted to lead us and teach us and share with us his companionship and grace. During the times I wandered off, when I tried to make my own trails, I missed out on experiencing these joys.

The path of Christ's endurance isn't all flowers and light, though. There are some really tough parts. We get tested; we become scared; we grow weary. Sometimes it feels like we aren't going to make it. We have to depend on his strength to keep going and persevere to the end of the trail. We can't do it by ourselves.

Most importantly, Jesus doesn't give up on us. No matter how far away we wander, he keeps his eye on us. He always knows where we are. He cares about us deeply and wants us to find our true freedom in him, not in running away.

And he is always holding out his hand to help us back.

INVITE HIM IN

If you are feeling lost, reach out for God's hand. He will help you back to the path of his love and endurance. It's not as narrow as you think. Jesus makes space for you to experience his grace, his strength, and the glorious destination of eternal life with him. He will be with you every step of the way.

PRAYER

Dear Jesus, please take me by the hand and lead me. I want to walk with you on the *path* of your merciful love and faithful endurance. Thank you for bringing me back, no matter how many times I try to go my own way.

LIFELINE

noun: a line used by astronauts and divers to keep
contact in a dangerous situation; something regarded
as indispensable for maintaining or preserving life

*We who have run for our very lives to God have every
reason to grab the promised hope with both hands and
never let go. It's an unbreakable spiritual lifeline, reaching
past all appearances right to the very presence of God.*
HEBREWS 6:18-19

I hope I never need one. A lifeline, I mean. I almost can't breathe when I think of how it would feel to be struggling in the water or floating in space without something to hold on to. No way to communicate or escape. Facing certain death unless someone throws a rope to me. I'll do everything I can to keep myself out of a situation that desperate.

But no matter how hard we try to stay safe, we can't prevent every bad thing from happening to ourselves or the people we care about. Sometimes we need help, support, or intervention to survive. That's why there are thousands of rescue organizations. Appropriately, many of them have the word *lifeline* in their titles. All of them provide critical services such as disaster relief, rehabilitation, suicide prevention, and the distribution of emergency food and water. Helping people, saving lives, and providing hope.

Hope.

Don't we all need it?

The promised hope of being rescued by Jesus is offered to everyone.

The lifeline he's holding out for us is available 24/7, no matter where we are or what we are up to. Easy to reach. A direct connection to God himself.

The hope that is given to us is unbreakable, unyielding, durable. It never weakens or fails. It holds firm and strong forever. Our verse for today words it this way: "reaching past all appearances." No matter what we see happening. No matter what we are worrying about. Straight from panic to peace.

The lifeline of hope that comes from Jesus anchors us securely. We will never be drifting alone or left to drown as long as we are holding on to him. What relief! What confidence and joy! He is our true Savior. He is the only one who can keep us safe. He is the only one who can rescue us from every doubt and fear and loss.

INVITE HIM IN

You don't have to struggle through this day, this life on your own. You don't have to save yourself. He is reaching out to you with indescribable hope and peace. He will keep you safe and strong. All you have to do is trust him. Grab this lifeline he offers with both hands. And then hold on tight and never let go.

PRAYER

Dear Jesus, thank you that I can count on you to save me. You pull me from fear to peace, from dark to light, from sin to grace, from desperation to joy. Thank you for your unbreakable *lifeline* of hope that keeps me secured to you.

HIDE

verb: to remain out of sight; to conceal for
shelter or protection; take cover

You've been a safe place for me, a good place to hide.
PSALM 59:16

Hiding. It was so much fun when we were kids. The space under the basement stairs with the tiny door and our favorite toys; the corner of the attic with sleeping bags and pillows, flashlights and books; the "fort" under the big tree in the front yard where no one could see us. It felt so safe and protected to be hidden.

But hiding for real—hiding because we are scared, exhausted, or threatened—is different. David wrote some of his most heartfelt psalms while hiding from Saul, who was determined to find him and kill him. He hid for years because his life was in real danger. And God was his safe place.

God is our safe place too. I remember beginning to believe this at 19. I was working for the summer at a Young Life camp in British Columbia, accessible only by boat or seaplane. It was protected there. The camp was alive with God's presence, with genuine people and spiritual conversations. The beauty was breathtaking—water, mountains, and sky all around.

Here I was at this incredible, God-filled place. Yet, I felt terribly afraid. Afraid of finding out who I really was inside. Afraid of the enemy and his evil schemes. Afraid of risking and losing, of grief and change. Afraid of the rest of my life.

I was not being pursued by a human enemy. I was not in real physical danger or escaping from a bad situation. I was just trying to accept myself and learn to trust Jesus with everything. And it was scary. It still is sometimes. But as I gradually started to turn my fears, my life over to him, God came close. He hid me in the shelter of his wings, held me close through the storms and darkness, and protected me. And he just keeps making me braver and stronger as I hide in him. He is my retreat. My escape. My perfect hiding place.

INVITE HIM IN

Let Jesus surround you. Ask him to give you a special hiding place. It might be a building like a church or cabin. It might be a peaceful place in nature like a beach or garden path. It might be a comfortable chair with your Bible and a blanket or a few minutes in your parked car to escape from the world. No matter where you are or how scared you feel, you are safe as you rest in him.

PRAYER

Dear Jesus, thank you for being my safe place. You are always here, covering me with peace and protection and love. Please let me *hide* in you right now.

Rooted

adjective: embedded, fixed, established, entrenched, ingrained

You're deeply rooted in him.
Colossians 2:7

As overwhelming as it is, I'm going to think about my garden for a minute. I'm going to be brave and think about weeding. Because when I hear the word *rooted*, I picture the little tree starts that infiltrate our yard from the seeds dropped by the huge maples and alders that surround us. The longer I wait, the tougher they are to pull out of the ground. Their roots are relentless, holding on to the soil for dear life.

Clinging to the soil provides everything necessary for energy and growth. Absorbing the water and nutrients strengthens the trees. Becoming established in the garden, digging in deeper every day, helps the trees grow up strong.

If we are rooted in Jesus, he will be our essential source. Our growth and strength will depend on him. As we trust him, as we "dig in" to a closer relationship with him, he will support and sustain us. He will provide us with everything we need.

> They're like trees replanted in Eden,
> putting down roots near the rivers—
> never a worry through the hottest of summers,
> never dropping a leaf,
> serene and calm through droughts,
> bearing fresh fruit every season (Jeremiah 17:8).

Along the river is where the soil is moist and the water is plentiful.

In a place where drought threatens and the heat is stifling, the trees planted by the water can thrive. They don't worry, even in the hottest times when the river is low. They can be calm and peaceful—continuing to grow and bear fruit *every season*.

Can we?

Can we trust him enough—the one we are deeply rooted in—to feed us and water us, strengthen us, support and establish us? Even when it's a stressful time, a painful time, a time of battles and fear that threaten our lives?

Yes, we can. Because the other incredible thing about roots is that as they get bigger and stronger, they begin to break through things that seem impossible to penetrate. Sidewalks, roads, cement walls, huge boulders. We may not realize it as it is happening, but eventually, we will see the results of the growth.

INVITE HIM IN

Spend a few extra minutes digging deeper into the rich soil of his love today. No matter what kind of drought you are facing, you can trust that as a believer you are planted by the river of God—the source of everything you could possibly need. He is your life and health and strength. He is breaking through things that you don't even know are in your way. And he is growing you stronger every day.

PRAYER

Dear Jesus, thank you for providing everything I need. Thank you that I can live confidently and peacefully knowing that I am *rooted* in you. I ask you to help me grow deeper, saturated and nourished by your never-failing truth and love.

TRUE

adjective: existing in fact and not merely as
a possibility, genuine, actual, real

*Summing it all up, friends, I'd say you'll do best by filling
your minds and meditating on things true, noble, reputable,
authentic, compelling, gracious—the best, not the worst;
the beautiful, not the ugly; things to praise, not things to curse.*
PHILIPPIANS 4:8

Sometimes the truth hurts. We all understand that. But believing things that are *not* true can hurt even more. Being misled, deceived, or even just wrong can be devastating.

Lies come from the enemy, the evil one. He uses false information, illusion, and trickery to confuse us and cause us to doubt. He wants to keep us from trusting Jesus.

He makes us doubt ourselves: *I'm really not worthy. I'm too weak. I feel like a fake. I do everything wrong. How can anybody love me? Does God even see me?*

He makes us doubt our God: *Did he really rise from the dead? Does he really hear our prayers and answer them? Can he really forgive every sin? Is the Bible true? Does he still do miracles? Is he really coming back again?*

All of us live with beliefs that bind us up in fear and insecurity—lies that hurt and negatively affect how we see ourselves and others. And all of us have experienced things that conflict with our understanding of Jesus. A prayer doesn't get answered the way we wanted; we can't seem to hear his voice; we question what seem like contradictions in the Bible; or we disagree with something stated by a Christian leader.

To counter these constant doubts and questions, Paul tells us to fill our minds with things that are true. Fill them up so there's no room for this devastating doubt. He encourages us to pack our minds full of the promises of God, the truths in his Word, the answered prayers, the faithfulness, the times when we have clearly experienced the presence of Jesus.

Paul urges us to think and pray and talk about the best things. The beautiful things. The praiseworthy things in this life. If we look for them, we will find them. If we focus on these positive, good, right things, our minds will clear. Our emotions will calm. Our loads will lighten.

And the truth will set us free (John 8:32).

INVITE HIM IN

Ask Jesus to help you focus on what is true and protect you from the enemy's hurtful lies. Let him fill your heart and mind with the best so there is no room for the worst. The truth is that he lived, died on the cross, rose from the grave, and is coming back again. He is good; he is faithful; he is love. You can count on him.

PRAYER

Dear Jesus, your truth sets me free. Please help me to fix my thoughts on the things of you—things that are pure, holy, right, lovely, excellent, *true*, and worthy of praise. I want my mind and heart to be filled up with you.

HEADLONG

adverb: plunging headfirst; recklessly,
carelessly, without thinking

I've thrown myself headlong into your arms.
PSALM 13:5

My husband and I have our own "episode" of *America's Funniest Home Videos* in our memories that makes us laugh out loud whenever we think about it. It involves our two-year-old son, a slippery pool deck, a hot tub, and a bright orange full-body flotation swimsuit with a sewn-in inner tube. Poor kid.

You can probably imagine what happened. It was our first day of vacation. Andy couldn't wait to get to the hotel pool. He wriggled away from my hand and started running toward the large hot tub full of unsuspecting people. Of course, he couldn't see the ground because of the unwieldy inner tube around his waist, and he was moving awfully fast. His tiny feet hit a slippery spot just before he was going to jump into the bubbling water, and he was immediately launched into the air. We froze, helpless, as we watched our little guy do an (unintentional) 360-degree, head-over-heels flip into the water. Somehow, he landed safely in the middle of all the hotel guests and came up smiling. It was horrifying and hilarious all at once. Thank you, Jesus, no one was hurt.

The word *headlong*. I get it now. And I love it.

The word makes me laugh, but it also calms my anxious heart. Because we all do things without thinking sometimes; we lack calmness and restraint when we commit to things and make decisions. We judge too quickly. We run too fast.

Or we do the opposite. We perseverate about things. We over-think, worry ourselves sick, and miss out on opportunities by being too careful. Sometimes we feel like a decision is too weighty or too complicated, so we just don't make one. We get stuck.

Yet, Jesus is always available. His loving, welcoming arms are ready whenever we are. And it's okay to come to him anytime, any-where, any *way*. Let's not think too hard about it or worry about approaching him with caution. We can just plunge in headfirst. He doesn't mind if we fall in exhausted or if we end up doing an acci-dental head-over-heels flip. He will catch us and hold us safely in his arms.

INVITE HIM IN

Go to Jesus. You don't have to prepare or plan out how you are going to be with him. You don't have to think hard about it. It's okay to be a little bit reckless and carefree this time. You can run to him like a toddler running to a swimming pool. Jump in and have some fun—he's right there waiting to catch you!

PRAYER

Dear Jesus, thank you for letting me run to you without reserva-tions. I just want to fall in *headlong*, knowing that I will land safely in your arms. I come to you now, trusting, delighted, and free in your love.

COURAGE

noun: strength of mind to carry on in spite of danger; bravery

Tell fearful souls,
"Courage! Take heart!
GOD is here, right here,
on his way to put things right."
ISAIAH 35:4

I love the Cowardly Lion. One of my favorite scenes in *The Wizard of Oz* film is when the wizard scares the lion so terribly that he turns and runs as fast as he can through a seemingly endless hallway and dives headfirst out a window.

Don't we all feel like this sometimes? *I'm such a coward. I'm too scared.* We want to run the other way fast.

Does it help to know that Jesus understands fear and anxiety? That he knows what it feels like to *try* to be brave? Luke 9:51 tells us that Jesus "gathered up his courage and steeled himself for the journey to Jerusalem."

He gathered his courage. He steeled himself for what was ahead.

Even Jesus had to find the strength to do something horribly difficult and painful. He did it, and now he helps us do it. He can empower our hearts because he knows exactly what we need.

The word *courage* comes from the Latin word for heart—*cor.* That's where we find courage when it's nowhere else. Our bodies may be shaking, our minds racing, our lungs gasping, but deep inside our hearts, where the Holy Spirit resides, we are brave. And we can face whatever is ahead—no matter how hard it might be—knowing that Jesus is right here with us.

INVITE HIM IN

Do you feel like a coward sometimes? Afraid, inadequate, tempted to run away? Ask Jesus to help you gather your courage. In your scariest moments, he is "here, right here." Trust that he is "on his way to put things right," and let his power and love make you braver than ever.

PRAYER

Dear Jesus, your heart strengthens mine and gives me *courage* for each day. Thank you for being brave, determined, and resolute during the hardest times of your life on this earth. Please keep me believing that you are always on your way to put things right for me.

Shoulders

noun (plural): the upper joints of the arm, the part of the
body that connects the upper arm to the trunk and neck

verb: to place or bear on the shoulder, to assume
the burden of responsibility or blame

Pile your troubles on God's shoulders—
he'll carry your load.
Psalm 55:22

I went purse shopping the other day. As I was browsing the different sizes and styles of bags, I overheard a woman telling her friend that she really prefers big purses, but her doctor had told her she couldn't use them anymore. The weight of her big purse was causing her serious problems with her shoulder. I felt sorry for her as I chose a rather large tote bag, thankful that my shoulders are still holding up okay.

Many people that I care about have had shoulder surgery. Through their experiences, I have learned that shoulders are extremely complicated joints made up of several bones, muscles, ligaments, and tendons. They are incredibly mobile—enough for the wide-range actions of the arms and hands—but strong and stable enough to allow lifting, pushing, and pulling. They can also hold a great deal of weight.

And God's shoulders are the strongest. His are the most mobile and stable of all. And luckily for us, he is offering to carry our load, our troubles, our heaviness...us.

So we can let him take them. Bags of shame and guilt, packs of pain, depression, and fear. We don't have to carry them anymore. He is offering to hold them for us as we walk through this life. He has already taken care of every single thing we think we need to haul around with us. Nothing is too heavy for him.

And if we need him to, he will even scoop *us* up and affectionately put *us* on his shoulders, just like a strong, loving, playful dad does with his child. Sitting up that high, held by our Father God, gives us a completely different perspective on everything that is going on around us. It makes us feel light and alive, safe and free.

Jesus tells us in Matthew 11:30, "Keep company with me and you'll learn to live freely and lightly." I think I want to depend on the shoulders of Jesus a lot more often.

INVITE HIM IN

Will you hand your heavy burdens over to Jesus? He can take care of them all, and more importantly, he can take care of *you*. Ask him to lighten your load and hold all your stuff. Or, simply reach up your hands. Let him put you on his shoulders for a while. He is more than strong enough to carry you through this day.

PRAYER

Dear Jesus, thank you for carrying my burdens, for taking my heavy load. Your *shoulders* are so much stronger and broader than those of anyone else I try to depend on. Thank you that you are more than able to hold the weight of my life today.

INDISPENSABLE

adjective: absolutely necessary, extremely
important, impossible to do without

God's Word is an indispensable weapon.
In the same way, prayer is essential.
EPHESIANS 6:17-18

Things I don't want to try to live without: coffee, flip-flops, toothpaste, my bed, dark chocolate.

The list of things I think I need is long and sometimes silly.

But air, water, food, and shelter...these are critical. We couldn't possibly forget about them, discard them, or think of them as optional. We cannot live on this earth without them.

They are indispensable, necessary for life.

And in our spiritual lives with Jesus, Paul tells us that there are just two critical things. Two things we absolutely need in order to grow and learn and simply *survive*: God's Word and prayer. A small list with huge implications.

God's Word. A weapon, he calls it. Not to attack others, of course, but to protect ourselves. It is the source of all truth and shows us the way to righteousness, peace, faith, and salvation. We don't have to fall victim to the lies and traps of the enemy when we are holding on to what God tells us is true. Let's read it, think about it, talk about it, and act on it. Often. Let's keep it close and ready, not buried, dusty, ignored, or forgotten.

Prayer. This is our private conversation time with God. What a gift to be able to talk to the God of the universe, the Savior of the whole world! And how incredible that he hears us and talks to us too. Our good and caring Father, our strong protector, our closest friend.

Prayer connects us to Jesus, so it is essential that we keep this conversation going. It keeps us growing and alive. Whispering alone in the dark; gathering with friends; bowing together as a congregation; singing in our cars; journaling our worries, questions, thanks, and praise...We can pray in many different ways, anytime, anywhere. It's so important.

INVITE HIM IN

You are his child. He loves it when you come and talk to him. You are always welcome. He has also given you a precious book with his message of life-changing love and truth. Hold tight to these indispensable gifts of God's Word and prayer. Use them all the time. In them, you will find everything you need: protection, wisdom, hope, peace, grace, and freedom. They will save your life.

PRAYER

Dear Jesus, I cannot live without you. Thank you that the words you give me and your faithfulness to hear me are forever. I will depend on your *indispensable* Word and prayer to guide my life.

Part Three

God's Faithfulness

Anyway

adverb: in spite of, regardless

*When everything was hopeless, Abraham believed
anyway, deciding to live not on the basis of what he saw
he couldn't do but on what God said he would do.*

ROMANS 4:18

Hopeless? Wondering how this pain, this struggle, this impossible situation can possibly work out? Do you want to believe that it will...even if you have every reason not to?

Abraham did. He dared to believe that God would be faithful to him and would keep his promise. "He didn't tiptoe around God's promise asking cautiously skeptical questions. He plunged into the promise and came up strong, ready for God, sure that God would make good on what he had said" (Romans 8:20-21).

He believed anyway, in spite of what he could see.

No matter how things appear to us right now, we can have that same kind of hope. The "plunging in" kind. Believing with all our hearts when we don't know what else to do. Why? Because God keeps his promises. Because he is who he says he is. And because every detail of our lives matters to him.

Are you stinging from that critical comment, that cruel social media post, that false accusation? *He can help you look for kindness and goodness...anyway.*

Disheartened by the stressful pace of life, the daily news, the pressures of school and work and home, the lack of time and sleep? *He can help you breathe in joy, peace, and laughter...anyway.*

Overwhelmed with fear about the health concern, the debt, the conflict that won't go away? *He can help you hold on to hope and trust in him...anyway.*

Life is not always "good" for any of us. But God is. Always.

INVITE HIM IN

Does God seem far away right now? Just start talking to him...anyway. Why? Because inviting him in can change things. It can change us. Like Abraham, let's decide to live not on the basis of what we see we can't do, but on what God said he will do. He promised that he will restore everything (see Acts 3:19-21). He promised that he will work all things together for good, even if what we can see right now is not (Romans 8:28). In spite of...regardless...he is good, and we really can trust him. Anyway.

PRAYER

Dear Jesus, even when what I see or feel or think tells me otherwise, I want to believe you *anyway*. Thank you that you are faithful to the end. I can trust you no matter what.

STICK

verb: to adhere or cling to; to remain in a place; to bind, unite

I'll stick with you until I've done everything I promised you.
GENESIS 28:15

Post-it notes are my favorite office supply. I have tiny neon ones, white poster-sized ones, star-shaped ones, heart-shaped ones, and ones of every color and size in between. I use the lined ones for grocery lists, reminders, bookmarks, and notes to my friends.

And what about Velcro? Don't we all use it to hold together shoes, jackets, backpacks, and hundreds of other things in our lives? Someone figured out that hooks and loops pressed together can create a bond strong enough for attachments even on space shuttle supplies. [2]

These might be kind of silly examples, but we really do depend on them. We need things to stick. We need people to stick. And even more importantly, we need God to stick.

In Genesis 28, Jacob learns that God is going to stick with him. In a dream, God reveals to Jacob that he intends to give the land he is sleeping on to him and his descendants. He promises to stay with Jacob and protect him. To bring him back home (verses 13-15).

Jacob woke up, and in verse 16 he says, "GOD is in this place— truly. And I didn't even know it!"

He didn't know it because he was preoccupied with his guilt and fear and exhaustion. He had deceived his father and cheated his brother. He was on a lonely journey, searching for a wife and sleeping on the hard, cold ground with a rock for a pillow.

But God looked past all that. He loved Jacob, and he had a better plan for him.

He does that for us too. He looks past all our distractions, right into our hearts. He finds us where we are and lets us know that he is with us.

Even when we mess up.

Even when we forget about him.

Even when we are running away from him.

Even when we don't really expect him to show up.

He sticks with us to the end.

INVITE HIM IN

Cling to God. He will be faithful to you no matter what is going on in your heart. Feeling guilty? Fearful? Lonely? Discouraged? Running in a thousand different directions? He is right there with you. Sticking with you, keeping his promises to you—whether you realize it or not. Let him hold you close today.

PRAYER

Dear Jesus, it comforts me to know that you are going to *stick* with me. You are always with me, protecting me wherever I go. Thank you for being my constant companion.

BRAVE

adjective: ready to face and endure
danger or pain; showing courage

Be brave. Be strong. Don't give up.
Expect GOD to get here soon.
PSALM 31:24

One of my favorite words is *brave*. Maybe because I really want to be. It seems so honorable to be brave. Anxious people like me admire first responders, servicemen and servicewomen, people who fight through diseases and tragedies with a positive spirit, and those who take huge risks like sailing across the ocean or climbing mountains. Or skydiving: free-falling out of a plane at 13,000 feet in the air. Counting on a piece of fabric and some ropes to save your life. The thought scares me to death.

What would it be like to be strong enough to face challenges like that with confidence despite the high possibility of failure or loss? I would love to have that kind of courage.

But I don't. On my own, I have a very tiny bit.

A lot has happened in the past few years of my life. I left the school community I had taught in and loved for 28 years and took a job at a brand-new kindergarten school near my home. I took a huge risk and started sharing my heart through my writing. My husband and I launched our first kid (now adult) out into the world, and the second one is close behind. I have experienced panic attacks, revisited some painful struggles from my past, and—hardest of all—I lost my beautiful mom to cancer. These changes have rocked my world more than I would like to admit.

I have had to get brave just to keep going.

I have realized that feeling scared doesn't mean I'm not brave.

I have had to depend on Jesus more than I ever have before.

And that's okay. Because he always shows up. I'm learning that he is right there with us in the scary stuff, the hard stuff, and the new stuff that we must be brave for. He knows everything we are going through, and he is not going to leave us alone. Ever. The braver we need to be, the closer he comes.

INVITE HIM IN

Reach for Jesus's hand. He is right there, ready to help you when you are scared. Look up to him and open your heart to all that he wants for you. Even when the risks and changes rock you to your core, he is faithful and will bring good out of your circumstances. Don't give up—he can make you brave enough for whatever you are jumping into today.

PRAYER

Dear Jesus, by myself, I am not very *brave*. Thank you that I can put my hope and trust completely in you. Please help me depend on you to be the source of my courage and the strength of my heart.

WAIT

verb: to look forward expectantly; to remain; to hold on

GOD takes the time to do everything right—everything.
Those who wait around for him are the lucky ones.
ISAIAH 30:18

We are mostly impatient people. After all, we have places to go, things to do...now! Stoplights irritate us. Being placed on hold frustrates us. We want our packages delivered in two days or less. And waiting on God is the hardest of all. We pray for direction, ask him for something, believe he will act. But we don't get an answer right away—or for what seems like a long, long time.

So we try to "look forward expectantly," "to hold on" to what we know and believe about God. We know that he hears us. He is faithful. He gives good gifts to his children. And he never fails.

So why does it take so long?

Because "God takes the time to do everything right." He doesn't rush anything. His timing is perfect, and it is not at all the same as ours. And sometimes it has more to do with *us being ready* than it does with *him being slow*. "Doing it right" is a gentle way of saying that God might have a bit of work to do in our hearts before he can give us his answers.

Aren't we lucky that he cares enough to do that? The most thoughtful, meaningful gifts are the ones he gives us in his perfect timing. Answers that come exactly when we need them are the ones we remember and hold on to. He knows not only *what* we need (and don't need), but *when* we need an answer and *how* he can prepare our hearts.

Something special happens when we wait on God. As he works in our hearts, we grow in character, compassion, patience, maturity, trust, and love.

Maybe we should stick around a bit. As Micah 7:7 says, "I'm not giving up. I'm sticking around to see what GOD will do. I'm waiting for God to make things right."

INVITE HIM IN

Ask Jesus to be with you as you wait. You might be waiting for something that worries you, like lab results or a job interview. Maybe you are waiting for something you are dreaming of, like a baby or a proposal or an acceptance letter. Even if you don't *feel* grateful in the waiting, thank him for where you are. You are in a unique time and space where God can do incredible work in your heart. Trust that he is taking the time to do everything right.

PRAYER

Dear Jesus, please help me to wait with a grateful, expectant heart. When I feel impatient or even ignored, I will trust that you know me better than I know myself, and your timing is perfect. Your answers are always worth the *wait*.

WHY

adverb: for what cause, reason, or purpose

Sometimes I ask God, my rock-solid God,
"Why did you let me down?
Why am I walking around in tears,
harassed by enemies?"
PSALM 42:9

Why do bad things happen to good people?

We have been asking that question forever. I asked it again the other day when I found out that the four-year-old sister of one of my students has cancer. Stage four.

Why?

I could list hundreds of things I don't understand that break my heart. We all could. Good, kind, innocent people have awful things happen to them. And our first reaction most of the time is to ask, "Why? Why would such a loving and powerful God allow these things to happen?"

And the uncomfortable answer is that we don't get to know right now. We realize that the evil in this world affects every single person, and none of us are exempt from suffering. Still, we want an explanation, a way to reconcile these things in our hearts. So we keep asking, "Why?" and God hears us every time.

As we wonder and wait, he holds us. And we think of a few more questions—like the ones reporters are supposed to ask about who, what, when, where, and how. There's a lot more to find out about every situation than just the *why*.

Whom have you put in my life to help me with this, God? Whom can I connect with?

What is true? What can I thank you for in this pain?

When have you brought me through struggles in the past? Please remind me of all the times you have been faithful to me.

Where is your light shining in this darkness? Where can I see your Spirit working?

How can you bring good from this? How can I experience your presence in my pain and grief?

And after all the questions, we can rest in his arms of love.

INVITE HIM IN

Ask Jesus whatever's on your mind and heart. Bring him your doubts, your confusion, your anger, your tears. Even if you don't get all the answers right now, you can trust that he will be faithful to bring good out of the difficulties. He will draw you close and hold you through whatever is going on. He is your rock-solid God in an unpredictable world. And sometimes, that is all you need to know.

PRAYER

Dear Jesus, thank you for understanding me, for having compassion and grace on me when I ask, "*Why?*" Please open my mind and heart and help me trust you in the hard things. Thank you for your gentle reassurance that you are in control and you are good.

HALFWAY

adverb: at or to a point equidistant between
two others; in the middle, partway

*GOD met me more than halfway,
he freed me from my anxious fears.*
PSALM 34:4

What do you think of when you hear the word *halfway*? I suppose it can be a good thing to be halfway to somewhere—halfway to graduation, halfway through the race, halfway home.

But halfway isn't such a great place if we get stuck there. It's not a great place if we stop, afraid or unmotivated to go on. Halfway across the street, halfway done with a project, halfway through a workout, halfway dressed. It's uncomfortable, even dangerous, to stay halfway too long.

Do you ever feel like you are only *halfway* to Jesus? Are you stuck in the middle of the street that leads to the life he has for you? Are you living in a sort of spiritual "halfway house"? Hanging on to old rules and comforts that keep you from living free and filled and strong?

I've been there. I know that unsettled feeling, that false sense of security. I've memorized Proverbs 3:5: "Trust in the LORD with all your heart and lean not on your own understanding" (NIV). I often get partway to trusting him, but then I fall back on what I feel. Or what I think. Or what I doubt. Getting past the halfway point can be so hard sometimes.

We all tend to hold back parts of ourselves from Jesus, often unaware of the danger we are in.

But God understands us. He knows that we get scared and hold on tight to our own control, our own understanding, our own ways. He sees us frozen in the middle of the street. He finds us hiding in our halfway houses, missing out on the life of freedom and joy he has for us. That's when he offers to come and meet us "more than halfway."

He will. Jesus loves us so much that he went all the way to the cross of pain and death for us. And he will continue to bring us all the way to him.

INVITE HIM IN

Tell Jesus that you feel stuck. Maybe you are scared. Maybe you are discouraged. Maybe you are worrying about what your friends and family will think, or you are just overwhelmed with life. He knows. He's reaching out his hand to bring you close. He wants to make you safe, complete, free. He has a dream for your life that is so much better than you can even imagine. Will you let him meet you where you are and bring you the rest of the way to him?

PRAYER

Dear Jesus, will you come and get me? I am stuck here in between where I used to be and where I want to be. I need your help to draw closer to you. Thank you that you will meet me more than *halfway*.

KEEP

verb: to cause to remain in a given place, situation, or condition; to watch over and defend; to take care of

Let's keep a firm grip on the promises that keep us going. He always keeps his word.
HEBREWS 10:23

We keep things. Special things like photos and books, treasured gifts, and handmade blankets. Valuable things like artwork and jewelry and electronics. Necessary things like legal papers and insurance policies and financial records.

These important things are what we take with us when we move. We keep them with us. We guard them. We don't ever want to lose them.

And God doesn't want to lose us. He is the master keeper. He keeps his promises. He keeps us going. He keeps his word.

And he keeps our hearts: protected, held together, close to him. He never lets us go.

He wants us to keep something too. He wants us to "keep a firm grip on [his] promises." He gives us promises that we can hold on to no matter what is shaking us up or tearing us down.

Some of my favorite promises are in 1 John 5:

- If we believe that Jesus is the Son of God, we can win out over the world's ways (verse 5).

- We can trust him. He reassures us with his truth (verse 6).

- We can know beyond a shadow of a doubt that God gives us eternal life through his Son, Jesus (verse 13).

- We can be bold and free in his presence (verse 14).
- We can ask him for anything according to his will, and he listens. He tells us that whatever we ask for is "as good as ours" (verses 14-15).
- We are held firm by God, protected and safe from the enemy (verse 18).

Here, in just a handful of verses, we get a glimpse of God's faithfulness, his love, and his fierce commitment to us. We start to realize the power he has to protect us and hold us.

I want to be kept by him. Don't you?

INVITE HIM IN

What's keeping you? If it's not Jesus, maybe it's time to let him free you, protect you, strengthen you, reassure you. You are more important to him than you can even imagine. He can keep you safe and cared for in his love and grace forever. He keeps his promises, and he will keep you. Will you let him?

PRAYER

Dear Jesus, thank you that you are so faithful, so good at keeping promises and keeping people. Help me to hold tightly to the hope you give. I trust you to *keep* me always.

STAY

verb: to continue in a place or condition; to stand firm, to remain

Now, children, stay with Christ. Live deeply in Christ. Then we'll be ready for him when he appears, ready to receive him with open arms.
1 JOHN 2:28

It sounds like a good place to stay, doesn't it? With Christ?

Jesus wants us to stay close to him. He wants us to stay grounded, stay steady, stay true, stay put. Not out of compulsion, but in loving response to his message of hope and grace and love.

But we aren't very good at it. Staying is hard for most of us. We are restless, busy, and easily distracted as we multitask our way through the day. We wander off mentally, physically, and spiritually.

So how can we get better at sticking around? How can we mentally, physically, and spiritually remain close to Jesus?

Mentally, we can picture ourselves sitting somewhere with Jesus, walking beside him, kneeling at his cross. We can read or listen to music or podcasts that help us think about his words of life, his stories, his miracles, his love for us.

Physically, we can look and listen for him in ordinary places. It might mean driving a different route in order to see the sunrise or sunset, looking out the window at nature more often, or maybe just going outside for a few minutes to breathe him in. We can start to notice his beauty and creativity everywhere.

Spiritually, we can have a running conversation with Jesus. We can just keep talking and listening to him all day long. It's easier to hear him, though, if we set aside a special time to pray, think about his words, or even just whisper his name.

We don't have to be formal. Reverent? Yes. Humble? Yes. Grateful? For sure. But we don't have to be in church to be close to him. Wherever we are, however we feel, whatever is going on around us, he is our closest friend. He is the one we can always talk to.

And when staying is hard for us, we can remember that he is the one who shows us how. He knows us, loves us, hears us, and faithfully remains with us forever.

INVITE HIM IN

Jesus is inviting you to stay with him. There is no safer, more comforting, more peaceful, or more exciting place to be than in his presence. Ask him to help you find your own special ways to mentally, physically, and spiritually stay close. He is standing right beside you in love and faithfulness to the end.

PRAYER

Dear Jesus, thank you for your faithful presence. Please keep me close to you, grounded and sure of who you are and what is true. Right beside you is where I want to *stay*.

ADVENTURE

noun: an exciting or remarkable experience;
a risky undertaking; quest

God, who got you started in this spiritual adventure,
shares with us the life of his Son and our Master Jesus.
He will never give up on you. Never forget that.
1 CORINTHIANS 1:9

A *dventure* is an exciting word most of the time. When someone tells their story of adventure, it usually involves elements of surprise and danger but ends well. If it doesn't, we call it something else, like a disaster or a tragedy.

But the story of Jesus's adventure from heaven to earth and back has a better ending *for us* than any we could even imagine...

The word *adventure* originates from the Latin *advenīre,* which means "to come toward, to arrive."[3] And if we shorten *adventure*, we end up with another exciting word: *Advent*. Advent: the season of expectation leading up to Christmas, the glorious day that we celebrate the arrival of Jesus.

God came toward us that day. He came *to* us. And he's determined to bring us back with him—to freedom, to healing, to redemption. He took a huge risk to come and get us, and he will never give up on his children. He will not leave us behind.

Because God loves us so much, he invites us to share in the life of Jesus. This spiritual adventure he offers us will be everything we are hoping for and more. And no matter how many twists and turns, disappointments or dangers we encounter, we can be sure that he will bring us safely home.

INVITE HIM IN

Tell Jesus you want to go with him. Something exciting is going to happen when you line up your heart and your plans with his. He is not going to let you live a boring life. He has crazy fun and huge surprises and unimaginable growth in mind for you. You will be challenged, uncertain, scared, and amazed on this journey with him. Don't be afraid; this is good news! Your adventure with Jesus will be worth the risk.

PRAYER

Dear Jesus, thank you for inviting me into this *adventure* of life with you. I am so excited and grateful to be part of your story of redemption and freedom and love.

SURE

God affirms us, making us a sure thing in Christ.
2 CORINTHIANS 1:21

I t feels so good to be sure.

There is a whole list of things that we are not so sure about these days. In times of transition and change, we start to feel unsure of our own security—our health, our finances, our relationships, ourselves.

"I'm not sure if I can do this."

"It's not a sure thing, but I'm hoping."

"I don't know for sure what's going to happen now."

We get insecure, become critical of ourselves and others, and second-guess our decisions. We lean this way, then that way...right, wrong, good, bad. We are just not sure.

But God "[makes] us a sure thing in Christ." That is encouraging news for those of us who worry. He affirms us; he is sure of us. He's our biggest fan.

We take a deep breath. God is sure of us? That makes us feel a little better. But there is so much uncertainty in our life of faith. We get confused about the rules, the denominational differences, the experiences that don't make sense, and the seeming contradictions in the Bible.

Does that mean we aren't sure of God? No. All we have to do is look up to him like a little one looks up to a loving adult. Big eyes, big faith, big dreams. Oswald Chambers put it this way:

> The spiritual life is the life of a child. We are not uncer-
> tain of God, just uncertain of what He is going to do

next. If our certainty is only in our beliefs, we develop a sense of self-righteousness, become overly critical, and are limited by the view that our beliefs are complete and settled. But when we have the right relationship with God, life is full of spontaneous, joyful uncertainty and expectancy. [4]

"Joyful uncertainty"? More confident in *who* we believe than in *what* we believe? That is the kind of sure that I want to be.

INVITE HIM IN

Just as he is sure of you, ask him to help you be sure of *him*. He wants to give you the kind of relationship that fills you with joy and trust and hope and fun. He will be faithful to you no matter how uncertain you are of him, your beliefs, your future, yourself. Because of Jesus, you are his, you are loved, and you are safe. For sure.

PRAYER

Dear Jesus, please help me remember that I can be *sure* of you when I start to doubt or fear. Thank you that you make me able to stand firm, hopeful and joyfully expectant because of who you are.

YET

adverb: at this time, until now, so far

It's what we trust in but don't yet see that keeps us going.
2 Corinthians 5:7

Not yet." That is not the answer we usually like to hear. "Are you feeling better? Have you heard from her? Did you get a call about the job? Have the test results come back?"

It's so hard not to know. "Not yet" as an answer to these questions can leave us feeling discouraged and fearful, wondering if what we are hoping for will ever happen. If it is not happening yet, how can we be sure that it ever will?

We can hope.

Many professions rely on hope. Educators, health care providers, coaches, therapists, and business owners have to believe in the *not yet*. The possibility of growth and change fuels their work. They keep trying, keep encouraging, keep improving. The word *yet* is powerful when hope is connected to it.

And those of us who know Jesus can move confidently from *hope* to *trust*. We have a relationship with the creator of the universe, the king of the world, the Savior of all. He knows what we need, what we are desperately waiting for, what we are struggling with. We can be absolutely sure that he hears us and will answer us faithfully. His answers always come—just not always in the way we are imagining. And usually not on our timeline.

Our hearts can get very heavy. We hurt deeply as illness, divorce, addiction, infertility, abuse, and grief threaten to destroy our lives and the lives of those we care about.

But when faith is attached to the *not yet*, it solidifies our hope. Even though we don't have all the answers right now, we can trust that they are on the way. We can live in the confident expectation that God is faithful and will come through. We can live by faith and not by sight. It's not just wishful thinking. It's real joy, lasting peace, and a deep breath of assurance and rest for our weary souls.

Faith in our Jesus—no matter what we see right now—will keep us going. He's got it all in his hands. He is making all things new (Revelation 21:5). He is working all things together for good (Romans 8:28). He just hasn't shown us everything he is working on...yet.

INVITE HIM IN

Ask Jesus to help you trust him, even when nothing seems to be working out. You can count on his faithfulness more than anything you see right now. There is so much to look forward to with Jesus. Take the leap from hope to trust as you wait for him. He always comes through.

PRAYER

Dear Jesus, thank you that you are the one I can trust in and base my life on. Even when I can't see what you are doing *yet*, please keep me going with the hope and faith that come from knowing you.

Part Four

GOD'S GRACE

FRESH

adjective: new, different, invigorating

*Now we look inside, and what we see is that anyone united
with the Messiah gets a fresh start, is created new.*
2 CORINTHIANS 5:17

He's alive!

That's what they discovered that first Easter morning. Lots of questions. Overwhelming excitement. And so much hope. If Jesus really was alive, then everything was going to be different. Everything was going to be new. *Fresh.*

Fresh just feels good. A breath of fresh air, a sip of fresh water, a freshly picked bunch of flowers, freshly washed sheets. Life-giving, energizing, clean.

The opposite of fresh is stale, old, spoiled. Like the discount produce section of a grocery store—gross. Nobody wants that stuff. And nobody wants to live like that. We get weary of the same old habits, dependencies, and unhealthy choices. We feel spoiled and stale and tired.

Jesus doesn't want that for us either. He rose on Easter morning and crushed the power of death to give us a fresh start. Together with him, we can be made clean and new and different, free from the things that drain us of our energy and joy.

INVITE HIM IN

Can you imagine being one of Jesus's followers on the morning that changed everything? You actually are. You can have your very own Easter morning with Jesus. You can ask him all your questions.

You can let yourself feel the excitement of what this new life will bring. And you can trust him to fill your heart with hope. Look inside the empty tomb, then look at Jesus. He *is* alive! Take the biggest breath of fresh air and ask him to make you new today. Everything can be different.

PRAYER

Dear Jesus, thank you for giving me a *fresh* start. Thank you for making a way for me to be united with you by dying on the cross. Please help me live freely in the joy and peace that come from this new life in you.

ENOUGH

adjective: as much as necessary, plenty, sufficient

My grace is enough; it's all you need.
My strength comes into its own in your weakness.
2 CORINTHIANS 12:9

If I made a list of everything I think I need right now, it would be awfully long. I've got a never-ending list of things I want too. Keeps me pretty busy, all this worrying about things I don't have.

I try to meet these needs in lots of different ways. Sometimes I turn to good things and helpful people. But sometimes I turn to not-so-good things and to people who might just tell me what I want to hear—instead of what is true and right. It's hard. And confusing. Until I remember that God wants me to bring *every need* to him.

So I do. I talk to him about what I need, what I want, and what I'm worried about. Sometimes I ask for direction, clarity, and help with a difficult situation. Often, I ask him to keep my family safe and healthy and happy. I ask for energy and patience and more of his presence in my life. And quite a bit of the time, I ask him to take away my weaknesses.

But then I read more of Paul's message in 2 Corinthians 12:9-10:

> Once I heard that, I was glad to let it happen. I quit focusing on the handicap and began appreciating the gift. It was a case of Christ's strength moving in on my weakness. Now I take limitations in stride, and with good cheer, these limitations that cut me down to

size—abuse, accidents, opposition, bad breaks. I just let
Christ take over! And so the weaker I get, the stronger
I become.

So maybe my list needs to be different. Maybe I should make a
list of things I am thankful for, including the hard things, even if I
don't understand why they are happening. Being grateful can change
us from needy to content, anxious to calm, weak to strong.

God knows exactly what we need. He sees our gaping holes, and
he pours his grace into them—filling them completely. Giving us
peace, giving us courage, giving us his kind of strength.

That's his grace. It is enough, "equal to what is needed." Just
exactly the right amount at the right time.

Enough for now.

Enough for this struggle.

Enough for you.

INVITE HIM IN

Bring your list of needs to Jesus. Thank him for his grace that
pours into us. Jesus does his best work when we let his strength
"move in on" our weakness. When we allow him to "take over." Let
him show you what his grace can do when you let him be everything you need.

PRAYER

Dear Jesus, you are *enough*. You fill my heart; you meet my every
need. Thank you for the perfect amount of grace that makes me your
kind of strong.

REAL

adjective: not imitation or artificial; actual, genuine, authentic

*What good would it do to get everything you
want and lose you, the real you?*
Luke 9:25

In Disney's magical version of *Pinocchio*, the lonely toymaker Geppetto wishes for his wooden marionette to become a real boy. Through a series of bad decisions and deceit, Pinocchio learns about being honest and unselfish and discovers his conscience. Ultimately, the mischievous marionette proves himself worthy and becomes a real boy.

But what about us? Like Pinocchio, do we find it easier to just go along with the temptation to run and hide sometimes? My nose starts to grow just thinking about the pretending I did today. I might have stretched the truth about how well things are going. I might have acted like I was fine, when honestly, I was desperate for a kind word. I might have said something with a passive-aggressive smile, when I was actually feeling angry and hurt. And I just might have talked behind someone's back instead of having an honest conversation with them.

We all pretend a little bit. We portray ourselves the way we want to be seen, the way we imagine that others think we should be. It's tricky. Because letting our world see just the smiling, capable, "always in control" us feels so much safer than just being real.

But it's not. We lose something valuable in the façade. We lose the opportunity to grow, to connect, to be known and loved for who we are. We lose relationships.

We lose ourselves.

But unlike Pinocchio, we don't have to prove ourselves worthy before we can be real. The real you, the real me is found in the grace-filled eyes of Jesus. Flaws? Yep. Failures? Those too. Fears and desires and struggles? He knows. And he created each one of us with a beautiful purpose that requires our genuine, unique, what-you-see-is-what-you-get, real self.

Jesus wants us to understand that there is nothing worth trading ourselves for. No approval, no job, no grade, no recognition, no image is worth that much.

He desires for us to experience being truly known and loved by him and by the people in our lives. Because of his open arms, his renewing spirit, his unfailing love, we don't have to pretend anymore.

INVITE HIM IN

Jesus is pretty taken with you—exactly the way you are. He understands that it takes hard work and a whole lot of courage to embrace the real you. Let him help you. He will reveal to you and everyone else the unique, creative, charming, authentic you who is so precious to him. You are loved, no strings attached. Really.

PRAYER

Dear Jesus, thank you that you know and love the *real* me. Help me always remember that nothing in this life is worth more than my relationship with you.

PERFECT

adjective: having all the required or desirable
characteristics; ideal, flawless

*It was a perfect sacrifice by a perfect person to
perfect some very imperfect people.*
Hebrews 10:14

The word *perfect* is in the Bible quite a bit—especially in this verse. It's used in conversation more and more too.

"Meet at 10:00?" "Perfect! See you then!"

"I found the perfect paint color for the hallway."

"The dinner was just perfect."

People say it without thinking, and we hear it all the time.

Even at Starbucks. I was in the drive-through line the other day, and I ordered my usual one-third decaf grande Americano with room. "Perfect," chirped the barista through the speaker.

Really? My coffee order was perfect? Huh.

Even though it was simply an expression of habit, I smiled. I liked hearing the word *perfect* attributed to something I did.

But I wish I didn't like it so much.

Perfect is a challenging word for people like me. People who strive for perfection are constantly criticizing themselves. Trying to please parents, teachers, bosses, spouses, kids, friends…that's way too many kinds of perfect to try to be. It's so defeating. Expecting ourselves to be perfect often comes dangerously close to destroying our bodies, our relationships, and even our souls.

Because we mess up. A lot. We act imperfectly most of the time. We say the wrong things, turn forms in late, forget appointments, stretch the truth, and disappoint people who are counting on us. The list of things we don't do exactly right is long.

But Jesus reminds us what kind of perfect we already are: *his* kind of perfect. Covered with grace, forgiven for every single mistake, and loved no matter what. His sacrifice washes away all the imperfect parts of us and makes us flawless in his eyes.

INVITE HIM IN

Give Jesus your discouragement, your disappointment in yourself. One by one or all at once, put your mistakes and regrets in his hands. He will get rid of them completely, continually, as often as you need. Ask him to show you how he sees you through eyes of compassion: imperfectly, *perfectly* his.

PRAYER

Dear Jesus, only by your perfect sacrifice can I enter your holy presence. Thank you that because of your precious blood, I am free and forgiven and new. Help me believe that I am *perfect* in your eyes.

EMBRACE

verb: to accept or support willingly and enthusiastically;
to welcome; to hold closely in one's arms

*The person who lives in right relationship with God
does it by embracing what God arranges for him.*
GALATIANS 3:11

n right relationship with God." We want *so much* to live that way. Unfortunately, we make it harder than we have to most of the time. We keep acting like the strength of the relationship depends on us, on our behavior.

But Paul tells us differently. In this same chapter (verse 5), he asks this question:

> Does the God who lavishly provides you with his own presence, his Holy Spirit, working things in your lives you could never do for yourselves, does he do these things because of your strenuous moral striving or because you trust him to do them in you?

Hmmm. That is a good question. What do we rely on most of the time?

- Our human efforts, or the awesome power of his Holy Spirit?
- Our limited ideas, or his infinite creativity?
- Our wishful thinking, or his ability to make all things new, to do miracles?

Clearly, God is the one who initiates everything that matters. He is the one who designs the pathways of our lives, the one who leads us to the relationships and opportunities that he desires to work in. He is the one who takes care of us with healing and grace, giving us courage and creativity and strength. He is the one who changes things, changes people. We cannot do that on our own.

And no matter how hard we try, we cannot make ourselves right with him.

So what do we do?

Embrace him. That's all. Embrace whatever he is arranging for us.

To *arrange* is "to make plans, to ensure that something is done by organizing it in advance."[5]

This is what God does. His Holy Spirit plans and orders things ahead of us, sometimes accomplishing the things that we might not have even thought of ourselves. He is always working, always orchestrating, always setting things up so that we can live and grow in a right relationship with him. He is in charge of making sure it happens.

Will we "willingly and enthusiastically" accept the gifts and challenges that he gives us? Will we trust him?

Will we welcome him with open arms?

INVITE HIM IN

Embrace Jesus. Take to heart his offer to make you right with him. He is the only one who can do this work. You can completely trust his plans for you. He ensures that good will ultimately happen in your life because he has organized it all ahead of time. Throw your arms around him and hold him tight. And remember, he already has his arms of love wrapped around you.

PRAYER

Dear Jesus, thank you that you did everything to ensure my salvation. Please help me trust you and *embrace* whatever you have in mind for my life. I wait with arms open wide for you!

BE

verb: to occupy a place or location, to have a
certain position; to have life, to exist

*Let's just go ahead and be what we were made to be,
without enviously or pridefully comparing ourselves with
each other, or trying to be something we aren't.*
ROMANS 12:6

I love cards. I love reading them; I love sending them; I love browsing
the card racks for the perfect design with just-right words. Today,
one caught my eye with its words in bold, pink print on bright yel-
low paper: "Just be you."

I wanted to buy it for everyone I know.

Because sometimes we get confused about just *being*. We count
on all kinds of things that don't belong in the definition of who we
are: how we look; what we've done; where we live, work, shop, or go
to school or church; what we eat or don't eat, drink or don't drink;
what other people think of us.

But God looks past all that. He sees who we really are, just the
way he made us. He wants us to peel off those outer layers one by
one and bring them to him. He wants us to trust him, letting him
take us to the heart of who we are and rest there.

He will help us be our real selves when we look to him instead
of everyone else.

We don't have to be afraid. We just have to start noticing...

Where am I right now? This community, this job, this family I am
part of—I just need to be here. Be present. Bring to this place, these
people the gifts that God has given me.

How am I right now? Tired, lonely, insecure, needy? Strong, capable, excited, creative? Probably a mix of both. I don't have to fake it, pretending I'm okay all the time. I can allow myself to feel. I can stop and breathe and ask for what I need.

Back to the card in the gift shop...I think God would want to send it to you. He wants you to know this:

You being you in him is much more important to him than *you doing things* for him.

You being you is his gift of freedom and grace. You don't have to prove yourself. You don't have to earn his love.

You being you means you don't have to work so hard. He has already made you beautiful, valuable, gifted with everything you need to live a life of love. Just be you.

INVITE HIM IN

Just be yourself with him. Trust him to do his beautiful work of revealing the real you. He made you, and he loves you more than you could possibly imagine. You are treasured, precious, cherished by him—just the way you are.

PRAYER

Dear Jesus, thank you that I don't have to earn your love. Please help me live in the joy of knowing that you made me and want me to *be* with you.

DESERVE

verb: to be worthy of; to earn, warrant, be qualified for

I don't deserve all the love and loyalty you've shown me.
GENESIS 32:10

Feelings of unworthiness. Lots of us struggle with them. We walk around believing that we don't deserve to be loved, valued, or cared for. We want those things so badly, but we know too much about ourselves. We get overly critical.

I haven't worked hard enough to earn a break, a treat, a massage, a nap.

I shouldn't have been given that compliment, that award, that gift. I don't deserve it.

I have no self-control. I should have never let myself eat, shop, drink, sleep in like that.

I'm not good enough, capable enough, perfect enough. Why would anybody go out of their way for me?

It's hard to accept anything good when we don't believe good about ourselves. But Jesus doesn't want us to beat ourselves up or put ourselves down. Isaiah 43 gives us a glimpse of how he sees us. Verse 1: "I have summoned you by name, you are mine." Verse 4: "...you are precious and honored in my sight." Verses 5-7: "I am with you...everyone who is called by my name, whom I created for my glory, whom I formed and made." He made us and he loves us. He sees good in us because he put it there. Our worthiness is from him—no matter what we've done, what we haven't done, or how deserving we feel.

And it's true that we don't deserve everything we get. That goes for good *and* bad things. Sometimes stuff just happens in life that we did nothing to cause or bring upon ourselves. We have to teach our kids early that life is not fair, because it really isn't.

One of my favorite scenes in a recent movie version of *Wonder Woman* made me think about Jesus. The battle between Wonder Woman (Diana) and Ares, the god of war, was intensifying, and we were on the edge of our seats. Ares was trying to destroy Diana physically as well as emotionally, so he told her that the people she was fighting for did not deserve to be saved.

Her response?

"It's not about deserve; it's about what you believe. And I believe in love."[6]

I think maybe Jesus is saying something like this to us. Will we believe him?

INVITE HIM IN

Bring your feelings of unworthiness to Jesus and let him wrap you up in his love. He will take your discouragement, your self-judgment, your insecurities, and give you grace and assurance in return. You are worth everything to him. He loves you, whether you think you deserve it or not. Believe it.

PRAYER

Dear Jesus, I confess my sin and selfishness to you and ask you to take it. Thank you that in spite of all the bad choices I have made, your grace toward me is unfailing. Help me accept and enjoy this love that I do not *deserve*.

BEST

noun: someone's most effective, capable, or successful
condition; the greatest degree of good or excellence

Look for the best in each other, and always do your best to bring it out.
1 Thessalonians 5:15

I like to think that we all try to do our best most of the time. Unfortunately, it's pretty common in our texting and emailing lives that something gets taken the wrong way. In fact, I would bet that every one of us has had at least one sent message misunderstood by the person who received it. Those misunderstandings are hard to repair. Sometimes we can't.

I wonder what Jesus thinks about all these messages that go zipping back and forth from heart to heart across his world. I'm pretty sure he told us his thoughts in the verse above: "Look for the best in each other." That sounds like a really good place to start. In fact, maybe that's the important thing. We should *start* there. Start by believing the best, assuming positive intentions, looking for the greatest degree of excellence in someone. If we are open to finding the good in that person, maybe we will.

We'll get disappointed by people for sure. There will be times when the message stings—and it was meant to. And as hard as it is to admit it, sometimes we are the ones who cause the disappointment and hurt.

Jesus understands our intentions, as altruistic or selfish as they may be. He sees us when we say something hurtful, gossip and criticize, and do things for the wrong reasons. He knows that we are sinners in need of a Savior.

And the best news is that he loves us still.

He starts with grace.

Let's start with grace too. Let's start by believing the best about ourselves and everyone else in our lives. Let's assume that everyone is doing the best they can as we all share in this time on earth together. And let's try to remember that we all interact in ways that are not the best sometimes.

Jesus tells us to "live out this God-created identity the way our Father lives toward us, generously and graciously, even when we're at our worst. Our Father is kind; you be kind" (Luke 6:35-36).

INVITE HIM IN

Ask Jesus to bring out the good, the best of you today. Ask him to help you forgive yourself and others for hurtful communications. Give him your conversations—the face-to-face ones and the ones that are sent from screen to screen. He will help you start each one with kindness and grace.

PRAYER

Dear Jesus, thank you for your forgiveness and compassion toward every single one of us. Please make me kind like you. Help me be gentle and forgiving, looking for the *best* in everyone I interact with today.

FLOW

verb: to move in a stream; to derive from
a source; to proceed smoothly

*His very breath and blood flow through us, nourishing us
so that we will grow up healthy in God, robust in love.*
EPHESIANS 4:16

My toes have a problem. Every once in a while, one of them turns white and goes completely numb. It's called Raynaud's syndrome. The temporary numbness is caused by spasms in the blood vessels which prevent the blood from circulating to the poor little toes.[7] It feels weird. And cold.

Blood flow is critical, even for the tiniest parts of us. If the vessels never opened back up, this minor toe problem would become much more serious.

Blood, water, air, electricity...we need these things to flow. We depend on them to be in motion. Moving from a rich and plentiful source, bringing things down or out or up to wherever they are needed. Important things. Life-giving things.

Fresh water flowing down from the mountains, giving life to the valleys below.

Electricity flowing out from the power station, bringing light and heat to the community.

Tree sap flowing up from the roots, delivering water, minerals, and hormones to each branch.

Blood and oxygen flowing out from our heart and lungs, bringing warmth, nourishment, and energy into every cell of our bodies.

But what about our spirits? What do we need for our hearts and souls to keep growing closer to him? And what about our weak, fearful, hidden parts? Can God send strength to these hard-to-reach places?

His life-changing blood can. His life-giving breath can too. If we open up to him, he will pour into us. Love and strength and healing flow continually from God above. Reaching every single part of us. Even our toes.

INVITE HIM IN

Take a deep breath and ask him to sustain you. His breath and blood will flow into you, filling you with everything you need right now. Comfort, calm, energy, patience, forgiveness, hope...he is your source. He will bring to even the tiniest parts of you exactly what's needed for you to grow closer to him. Allow his love and warmth and light to flow in you and through you today.

PRAYER

Dear Jesus, thank you that you are the living, moving, healing God. You constantly bring me what I need to grow stronger and healthier and closer to you. Please let your Spirit *flow* freely through me today.

Unforced

adjective: done or produced naturally,
not compelled or constrained

*Walk with me and work with me—watch how I
do it. Learn the unforced rhythms of grace.*
Matthew 11:29

'm behind again. Staying up late, multitasking constantly, trying to
get everything done. Why does it seem that the harder we try, the
faster we go, the more we force ourselves...the less we accomplish?

Jesus sees us—his tired and defeated friends. He wants to help
us find a balance of work and rest and effort and trust. He wants to
teach us his rhythms of grace. He asks us to walk with him and work
with him and watch him.

Walk? Maybe instead of rushing around to this frantic beat, running at high speed and volume, we can get in step with Jesus. He is
not in a hurry. He can help us breathe and notice his gifts as we pace
ourselves alongside him.

Work? Yes, we have a lot to do. Jesus knows everything that's on
our lists. In fact, he put some of it there. Work is important, fulfilling, necessary. It's not a bad thing unless we forget to stop and rest
and play. And pray.

Watch? Jesus is our example, our mentor, our guide. He will show
us how to do this busy life without losing our minds or souls. We just
need to keep our eyes focused on him.

Jesus did the most important work in history. But he didn't force
anything. He taught, built, healed, traveled, invested in people, took
care of details, led a small group, and still made time to get away and

pray and rest. He was so in tune with God that he was able to bring calm to times of stress. There was a peaceful, genuine, natural flow about his life, kind of like music.

Songs are beautiful combinations of melody, beat, tempo, volume, style, and rhythm. The rhythm is key. We listen to slower songs when we feel quiet or thoughtful, and faster songs when we're upbeat and energetic (or trying to be). Maybe we can let him take us through our days like the rhythm of a song.

INVITE HIM IN

Ask him to help you walk with him, work with him, and watch him. He wants to be with you as you go through this day. Busy stretches, quiet moments, the ebb and flow of your routine. Like a beautiful piece of music, let his rhythms of grace help you find balance and joy, energy and peace.

PRAYER

Dear Jesus, I want to walk with you and work with you today. I am exhausted from trying to keep up with my life, and I need you to set the pace. Please be close to me, slow me down, and help me live in your *unforced* rhythms of grace.

FOUND

adjective: discovered after a deliberate search;
located, recovered, brought back

Imagine a woman who has ten coins and loses one. Won't she
light a lamp and scour the house, looking in every nook and
cranny until she finds it? And when she finds it you can be
sure she'll call her friends and neighbors: "Celebrate with me!
I found my lost coin!" Count on it—that's the kind of party
God's angels throw every time one lost soul turns to God.
LUKE 15:8-10

One of my most vivid childhood memories involves me standing in church next to my mom singing the words to "Amazing Grace": "I once was lost, but now am found; was blind, but now I see."[8]

I remember thinking that I was glad I wasn't really lost *or* blind. I wondered why we were singing about that, but I was pretty sure that everybody in those simple wooden Lutheran pews was in agreement that the grace of God was amazing. And that we needed some of it.

Yes, we really did. And we still do. Because we *are* lost without Jesus. The words of that beautiful old hymn still ring true.

Being lost is one of the worst feelings a human can experience. To be lost from our people, no matter what age we are, is terrifying. All the worst emotions pulse through us at once: panic, the pain of abandonment, confusion, despair...It's hard to breathe.

Spiritually, though, we don't always realize when we are lost. We don't always have a clear indication that we have become separated from our Savior. Maybe, like in my early years of church, we just haven't learned enough about him yet to know that we want to be found by him. It might be that we were close to him in the past, but now we have gotten distracted and wandered away. Or possibly, the doubts, fears, and circumstances of our lives have caused us to hide from him on purpose.

"I once was lost..." We all were. Some of us still are. That's why Jesus comes to find us. He looks everywhere for us, scouring every nook and cranny of the world. He doesn't give up, having even given his life to recover us, to bring us back to him. And when he finds us? The joy and relief of being found is overwhelming. We get to experience being loved, valued, cared about, and redeemed by him.

INVITE HIM IN

Turn to Jesus. Whether you believe it or not, you mean everything to him. Cry out to him, let him know you are ready to be found. He will find you, and he will bring you back. He'll save you with his amazing grace.

PRAYER

Dear Jesus, thank you that I have been *found* by you over and over throughout my life. Every time I have wandered away from you, you have brought me back with a celebration of genuine joy and relief. I am so grateful for your amazing grace.

Part Five

God's Generosity

STEEP

verb: to soak in a hot liquid; to cause
to become filled or saturated

Steep your life in God-reality, God-initiative, God-
provisions. Don't worry about missing out. You'll find
all your everyday human concerns will be met.
MATTHEW 6:33

This was the message I heard at a Young Life camp the night I gave my heart to Jesus. The speaker used today's verse to challenge us to give Jesus first place in our lives: "Seek first His kingdom and His righteousness, and all these things will be added to you" (NASB).

I was excited and terrified at the same time. Put God first? Above everything else that I loved and wanted in my life? Something deep down in my teenage heart was brave enough to say yes to that. To him. I wanted nothing to be more important to me than Jesus.

But putting him first has turned out to be a bit of a messy process for my selfish heart. It sounded so simple at first, but more often than not, my own desires have taken over. Too many times, I have climbed into that place of priority and bumped Jesus out of the way.

I've worried far too much about my family, about money, about my appearance. I've spent an inordinate amount of time and effort seeking the approval of others. And I've made some really important decisions in life without listening to him.

I keep learning that I have to continually, sincerely relinquish control and self-seeking. He is more than able to handle all the complicated parts of my life...of me. I just have to let him. It's that simple.

The process kind of reminds me of making tea.

It isn't difficult to do. Boil water, pour it into a mug with the tea bag, wait. But what happens during the waiting is really kind of fascinating. Hot water swirls over and through the tea leaves, creating streams of rich colors, delicious scents, and interesting flavors. In this intricate process, the heat and water transform dry, crumbling leaves into healing and comfort. It's beautiful.

And so it is with us when God has first place in our lives, when we are "steeped" in him.

His reality? A way bigger picture, a happy ending. Help and hope no matter what.

His initiative? Always love. Overwhelming grace. Bringing good into every situation.

His provision? Everything we need. More than enough. We really can trust him.

INVITE HIM IN

Steep yourself in his presence for a few minutes. Let him pour over your heart and saturate you with his grace and love. He will reveal the essence of you in the most beautiful, creative ways. And he will soothe your soul. You will have everything you need when you give him first place in your heart.

PRAYER

Dear Jesus, I want you to have first place in my heart. Please help me trust you in every situation to provide all that I need. I want to be *steeped* in you today.

RECEIVE

verb: to get or be given something; to react
in a specified way; to welcome

Receive and experience the amazing grace of the Master,
Jesus Christ, deep, deep within yourselves.
PHILIPPIANS 4:23

The annual card from our sponsored child in Bolivia arrived the other day. She is old enough now to draw cute little pictures for us, like the one she sent of a girl, a rabbit, and a Christmas tree with a gift next to it. Translated below the drawing, we found this sweet, simple message from her:

"Receive lots of blessings of God."

"Lots of blessings of God"? Yes, he does give us lots. All the time. But do we really know how to receive them? This tiny little girl across the world might be reminding us of something extremely important. Maybe she's reminding us that receiving is an action—that it's something we *do*. And it matters how we do it.

It's kind of like when the UPS truck is parked outside the house and somebody dressed in brown sets a box on our porch. The doorbell rings, and we look at each other with curious faces, trying to remember what we ordered.

Our choices:

1. Leave the box on the porch.
2. Take the box inside but wait to open it.
3. Open the box immediately—pulling off the tape and ripping the cardboard apart.

When God gives us blessings, we have these same choices.

Maybe he wants to give us a new experience that will strengthen our faith. Maybe he is providing an unexpected opportunity that will refresh our spirits. Maybe he has a creative idea to plant in our hearts, or a person for us to meet who will draw us closer to him.

What will we do when God comes bearing gifts? We might choose option 2 and wait a little bit. Or we could choose option 3 and eagerly begin to enjoy them right away. Maybe our sweet sponsored child just wanted to remind us not to choose option 1, not to leave God's blessings unopened on the porch of our hearts.

Let's take these blessings in with joy and expectation. Let's actively receive these gifts from God and experience his amazing grace deep, deep within ourselves.

INVITE HIM IN

Jesus is at the door of your heart with all kinds of packages. He has so many blessings for you—things you want and things you need—all wrapped up in his amazing grace. He's chosen them just for you. Ask him to help you receive your gifts with gratitude and joy.

PRAYER

Dear Jesus, I welcome you into my heart right now. Please help me gratefully *receive* the blessings you have for me today. Thank you that whatever you give me comes wrapped up in your grace and love.

SET

verb: to place with care or deliberate purpose

He thought of everything, provided for everything we could possibly need, letting us in on the plans he took such delight in making. He set it all out before us in Christ.
EPHESIANS 1:8-9

One of my chores growing up was to set the table for dinner. With minimal effort, my sister and I would gather the necessary tableware and condiments and place them on the dining room table. We didn't think it was very fun or important—especially when we had to get up from watching whatever was on TV.

But it *was* fun when we got to do this for holidays, birthdays, or company. To set an extra-special table with thoughtful details, nice dishes, and a favorite meal. Cloth napkins, place cards, flowers, plenty of food, and lots of joy to go around.

And Jesus? He has so much fun doing this for us. With care, deliberate purpose, and beautiful intention, Jesus sets before us the most inviting table we could ever imagine. He thinks of me and you as he designs the place settings and plans the meal. He knows what we need. He knows what we hope for. He knows what fills our hearts and satisfies our souls.

What holiday does he do this for? Whose birthday? What special occasion?

It is simply this—he has invited us to dinner. An ordinary day turns into a celebration when we accept his invitation. We are his company, his honored guests, his precious kids. He knows that we are weary and hungry for something more. And he can't wait for us to experience all that he has set before us. He wants to treat us to his very best—no expense spared, no detail overlooked. Exactly what we need and more than we could ever hope for will be on that table.

Love? Bowls upon bowls full—plenty to go around.

Peace? Quench your thirst with his unlimited supply.

Grace? It's the main course. Everybody gets a huge helping.

Hope and joy? Baskets overflowing. You can have as much as you want.

Wonder? Wait until you taste dessert! He has such amazing adventures in store for you.

INVITE HIM IN

Just for a moment, sit with Jesus. Allow him to give you everything you need and surprise you with more. Take in the food, the drink, the laughter, and the love at his table of grace. Come and relax in the special place he's saving just for you. It's all set.

PRAYER

Dear Jesus, thank you for a place at your table. Thank you for all you have prepared just for me. I want to sit with you and enjoy all the kindness, the forgiveness, the wisdom, and the abundance of grace in this day that you have *set* before me.

MULTIPLY

verb: to increase greatly in amount or number;
to become much more; to expand

*May GOD...keep it up and multiply you another
thousand times, bless you just as he promised.*
DEUTERONOMY 1:11

There are two stories in the Bible about Jesus feeding huge crowds of hungry people. Both times, all he had to work with was several loaves of bread and a few fish. Barely enough for a small family to have a picnic.

But Jesus wasn't worried. He thanked God as he held the small portions of food—trusting him to do something amazing. To "increase greatly" what was brought before him. To do much more than anybody expected. To multiply the tiny offering.

And God absolutely did. Thousands ate all they could—and still, there were baskets full of bread and fish left over.

I brought something difficult to Jesus a few months ago. I didn't know it at the time, but it turned out to be a multiplication problem. Some of the students I teach face challenges and situations that truly break my heart. I found myself worrying quite a bit about them, focusing on their problems, feeling discouraged. Hopeless. Even angry. I asked Jesus to help me with these tough emotions, these precious kids.

The answer he gave me involved a basket. (Of course it did!) A wise friend of mine encouraged me to write the names of the students I am concerned about on little pieces of paper, put the papers into a basket, and pray for the kids whenever I start to worry. Even though I can't do much to change the situations they are in, I know the one who can. He knows all their names, and he knows their stories. And even though I may not get to see the answers or the resolutions of the problems that these children are facing, I know the one who hears my prayers for them.

And he still does miracles. My little basket of hope has become a daily reminder that God can take my offering of faithful prayer— simple and small and seemingly not enough—and multiply the good in the lives of these kids. He can greatly increase the healing, the love, the resources, the answers they (and we) all need.

INVITE HIM IN

Ask Jesus to multiply your faith. Give him your prayers for change, your hard work in difficult places, your simple offerings. He wants to do miracles in the little bit that you turn over to him. Bring him your basket and let him overflow your world with everything you need. And don't be surprised if there is plenty left over.

PRAYER

Dear Jesus, please help me trust you in every situation. I bring to you my baskets of need, my hurting friends and family, my doubts and fears. Thank you that you will be faithful to *multiply* the little bit of faith that I bring to you today.

SHOWER

noun: an enclosure in which a person stands
under a spray of water to wash

verb: to give a great number of things
to someone; to heap or lavish

*God has us where he wants us, with all the time in this world and
the next to shower grace and kindness upon us in Christ Jesus.*
EPHESIANS 2:7

Sometimes we just need a shower. It feels amazing to step in dirty
and come out clean. To step in sweaty and sticky and come out
refreshed and cool. To step in freezing and come out warm and
relaxed. To step in sleepy and come out wide awake. A shower can
turn our day around.

We can also be "showered" with gifts by people who love us.
Bridal showers or baby showers are given to celebrate special life
events. Friends and families gather to generously "shower" presents,
attention, advice, and good wishes on the bride and groom or the
parents-to-be.

I like the water kind of shower, and I also like the party kind.
When I think of Jesus "showering" us with grace and kindness, they
both work.

The water kind of shower? We choose to get in. There, Jesus can
pour over us streams of grace and kindness, cleansing our hearts,
making us new, refreshing us, energizing us to live the life he calls us
to. We put ourselves into a place where he can turn our hearts, our
days, our lives around.

The party kind of shower? God plans these for us! He sees us in a

113

place of need or entering into something new. He lavishes upon us his attention and encouragement and strength. He gives us meaningful relationships, creative ideas, real peace, incredible beauty, and enduring hope. He is all about celebrating us and supporting us, whatever stage of life we are in.

INVITE HIM IN

You can ask Jesus for whatever kind of shower you need today. Maybe you need to put yourself in a place where he can cleanse your heart and renew your spirit. Maybe you need to warm up, cool off, wake up, or be refreshed. Maybe you are just feeling like you want to be taken care of—needing some attention, advice, support, and love. Let him pour down upon you his gifts of grace and kindness. He's got the perfect kind of shower for you.

PRAYER

Dear Jesus, thank you for *showering* me with the incredible wealth, the incomparable riches, and the extraordinary greatness of your grace. I am clean, refreshed, and overwhelmed by your goodness to me. Please help me live in this generous love today.

Extravagant

adjective: very fancy; more than is usual, necessary, or proper

Mostly what God does is love you. Keep company with him and learn a life of love. Observe how Christ loved us. His love was not cautious but extravagant.
Ephesians 5:2

There is a home (a skyscraper, really) in South Mumbai, India, that is worth over a billion dollars. A family of four lives in this monumental place with approximately 100,000 square feet of living space *per person.* Twenty-seven floors, nine high-speed elevators, three helipads, and six floors of underground parking for the fleet of one hundred sixty-eight cars. Most of the lighting and features in this mansion are made of marble, crystal, and mother-of-pearl. It has a full-size movie theater and a two-story recreation center with gyms, pools, and a "snow room" that creates man-made snow flurries to cool the residents on the hottest days.[9]

Expensive, fancy, more than is necessary. These don't seem like Jesus words. In my observations of Scripture, he appeared as such a humble, work-with-his-hands, no-worldly-possessions kind of guy.

So, was Jesus—*is* Jesus—extravagant?

Is he someone who thinks of things that would make life unbelievably better? Is he someone who wants the absolute best? Is he someone who exceeds expectations, goes above and beyond, holds nothing back?

Yes, he is. Not for himself, but for us. Not with possessions or riches, but with goodness, mercy, and peace. And most of all, Jesus is extravagant with his love.

He gladly pours his Spirit into us and fills us beyond what our hearts can hold. He overwhelms us with more than enough beauty and creativity and power to know him and live for him. He gives us more than is usual, more than is necessary, more than we can even imagine.

He doesn't have to be cautious, because he never runs out of love.

INVITE HIM IN

What do you need him to lavish upon you? What area of your life, your heart needs to be indulged, cared for, spoiled? Go ahead—ask him. Faith, courage, forgiveness, hope, healing, energy, direction...he has more than enough for you right now. Let him love you extravagantly today.

PRAYER

Dear Jesus, thank you that you love me more than I can possibly imagine. You showed me how to love by offering yourself as a sweet and beautiful sacrifice to God. Please make me more like you. I trust you to help me be *extravagant* in the way I love the people you have placed in my life.

OPEN

adjective: unblocked, unobstructed, available, receptive

Build yourselves up in this most holy faith by praying in the Holy Spirit, staying right at the center of God's love, keeping your arms open and outstretched, ready for the mercy of our Master, Jesus Christ.
JUDE 1:20-21

My husband and I love to ride bikes. One of our favorite places to ride is on the San Juan Islands in Puget Sound. One colder-than-usual fall day, we rode 17 hilly miles, looking forward to a treat at the Olga General Store on the far side of Orcas Island. We knew their homemade pie was fantastic, and it would be worth the long, cold trip. We were tired and hungry as we approached the store and read the sign in the window: "Closed for the winter."

The word *closed* felt like a punch in the stomach. After all our hard work and anticipation, we were awfully disappointed. Of course, we regained our perspective and started back toward the ferry. It was only pie, after all.

But isn't it so much harder when the disappointment happens to our hearts, our souls, our families, or our futures? When a job or a relationship doesn't turn out the way we hoped. Or when a dream is clearly not going to be realized. Once, God said no to something I really thought he was going to give me. As I lay in bed that night, tearfully questioning and wondering why, I decided to literally open my hands. I released my disappointment, trusting him for whatever he might want to do instead.

Almost a year later, the very thing I had wanted before happened in a much bigger, much better way. God's amazing-grace kind of way. He caught me by complete surprise and overwhelmed me with joy. I honestly believe that if I hadn't released my desires to him, I would not have been able to receive this incredible blessing.

He has so much to pour into us. But we've got to make ourselves available. We've got to be open.

If we open our eyes, he will show us things we could never have imagined.

If we open our minds, he will teach us. He will help us grow.

If we open our hearts, he will heal us, soften us, lead us in love.

If we open our hands—even when we don't feel like it—he will not let us down.

INVITE HIM IN

Open up to Jesus. Make yourself available right now and give him access to all of you. Let his Holy Spirit pour his beautiful, surprising gifts into your open places.

PRAYER

Dear Jesus, I want to trust you with my uncertain future, my disappointed heart. Help me remember that a closed door is never the end of my story with you. Thank you that you will generously fill my open eyes, my open mind, my open heart, and my *open* hands with your goodness and love.

SPLASH

verb: to cause a liquid to spatter about especially
with force; spray, sprinkle, slosh

May the Master pour on the love so it fills your lives
and splashes over on everyone around you.
1 THESSALONIANS 3:12

One of the most beautiful places in the Pacific Northwest is the Oregon coast. I love to go there when storms are likely and the waves are wild. Walking along the beautiful stretch of beach is an adventure in avoiding the puddles and streams in the sand. It's fun to jump over them, trying (but usually not succeeding) to keep my shoes dry.

Last time I was walking there, I noticed a family with two little girls bundled up in warm jackets and rain boots. They were not jumping over the deep parts like I was. They were jumping *in* them. Splashing water everywhere. And they were having the best time. Because splashing is pretty fun. Playing in the water, making it jump and dance and fly...and getting other people wet whether they like it or not.

In this verse, Paul is encouraging us to splash people—not with water, but with the love of Jesus. His love pours onto us like a waterfall. Graceful yet powerful, breathtaking and refreshing at the same time. He continually fills us to overflowing so that we can love others with this tangible, thoughtful, grace-filled love.

But we have to get into the water and move around in it to make it splash. We have to let him love *us* so we can share this love with others.

Let's put on our boots and jump in.

Let's talk to him, read about him, pray to him, worship him, and begin to truly experience his overwhelming love for us. Let's spend time soaking him in, letting him soothe our broken places and our hurting parts. Let's relax in the pool of his grace and creativity, trusting him to bring goodness and peace into our homes, our work, our relationships. Let's stand under his downpour of endurance and strength when we just don't feel loving at all. Only he can saturate us with the amount of love we need for ourselves and others.

INVITE HIM IN

Thank Jesus for his love that never stops flowing. Ask him to help you feel it soaking deep into your soul, healing your heart, giving you strength and refreshment. Ask him to open your eyes to the people around you who need a splash of his love and grace. And then let him love people through you in amazing, creative, and tender ways. Don't be afraid to get your feet wet! With Jesus, it's going to be fun.

PRAYER

Dear Jesus, thank you for your abounding love. Please help me *splash* in it every day. Make your love for me overflow with abundance—more than enough to share with everyone in my life.

ENERGY

noun: the physical or mental strength that allows you
to do things; a dynamic quality, a spiritual force

*Be energetic in your life of salvation, reverent and
sensitive before God. That energy is God's energy, an
energy deep within you, God himself willing and
working at what will give him the most pleasure.*
PHILIPPIANS 2:12-13

I use the word *tired* way too much. Sometimes I mix it up and use
the words *exhausted* or *wiped out*. Because I am. And so is just about
everyone I know.

We work hard, play hard, and run ourselves ragged trying to
get everything done. We have errands, paperwork, chores, appointments, and meetings. We take care of the things we have to, squeeze
in the things we want to, and hardly ever get enough sleep.

We get depleted. We run out of the physical and mental energy
that we need to get everything done.

But even though we can't always generate the level of energy we
would like to have, we *can* always draw upon the unlimited spiritual energy that comes from belonging to Jesus. That's God's energy
deep within us. God himself providing the motivation, the stamina,
the follow-through we need to live this life in a way that matters. We
really can't find it outside of him.

In the verses following today's passage, Paul encourages believers
to "do everything readily and cheerfully" (verse 14). He adds, "Provide people with a glimpse of good living and of the living God"
(verse 15).

That requires a lot of energy. To live in a way that glorifies him, in a way that brings good and love to our world, we need a constant charge from his Holy Spirit directly into our hearts, our minds, our bodies. With his energy and love, we can do whatever he asks us to—and maybe we can stop talking about how tired we are.

Let's not make it so hard. Living for Jesus isn't just *one more thing* we have to do, *one more thing* to find energy for. It's more like being carried by a wave, by a spiritual force that moves us when we lift our feet up and relax into it. When he is our source, the things we say and do have a dynamic, lasting quality. The ways we represent Jesus can have powerful, life-changing effects.

We've got all the energy we need deep within us. Let's depend on him.

INVITE HIM IN

Ask Jesus to make the difference in your energy level today. Lean into him. He will supply you with everything you need to work and play and be present with people. He will sustain you and strengthen you, especially when you need him the most.

PRAYER

Dear Jesus, thank you that you are the source of my *energy*. You give me the desire and the ability to do what you ask of me. Please help me feel this powerful connection to you today.

DIMENSIONS

noun (plural): the total amount of measurable space or surface occupied by something; size, extent, magnitude

I ask him that with both feet planted firmly on love, you'll be able to take in with all the followers of Jesus the extravagant dimensions of Christ's love. Reach out and experience the breadth! Test its length! Plumb the depths! Rise to the heights! Live full lives, full in the fullness of God.
EPHESIANS 3:17-19

My husband has been walking around our family room with a tape measure lately. We are thinking of buying a new television for each other for Christmas, and we are stuck on the size. Stuck because we have to fit the new TV into a cabinet that isn't nearly as big as the screens we are drawn to at the electronics stores.

Deep down, I want to get rid of the cabinet. I want to start over with new furniture and mount the television on the wall. That way, we would not have to keep trying to fit it into a specified opening.

Words like *dimensions, measurements,* and *specified* seem to box us in. Yet we rely on them so much. Our brains want to know the limits of things, the exact extensions in all directions and where they stop.

We do this with God's love too. We create a cabinet of a certain size and keep him in it. We imagine his love being incredibly good and wonderful, but only to a certain point.

His love reaches me until...
His love reaches me, but not if...
His love reaches me, except when...

But these limits? They are ours, not his. Our brains try so hard to

123

understand his unconditional, merciful love, but we just can't. His love will never fit into the dimensions we are working with.

What if we *do* get rid of the cabinet? What if we start to reach out and experience the breadth of God's love? What if we really try what today's verse encourages us to do—test its length, plumb the depths, rise to the heights? What if we open our hearts to the fullness of life that he has for us, trusting him to love us without measure?

Let's let his incomprehensible love reach way beyond our specifications.

Invite Him In

Ask God to help you expand your heart and mind. He wants to fill up a much bigger part of you than you've imagined with his grace, peace, joy, and hope. He wants you to live in this fullness without being afraid of it coming to an end. Absolutely nothing can keep you outside his love. Let him free you and relax you as he loves you without limits.

Prayer

Dear Jesus, thank you that your love reaches far beyond any earthly *dimensions*. How exciting that your love is greater than anyone can ever know completely! I desperately want to be filled beyond my limited understanding with all the fullness of you.

INVITE

verb: to request the presence or participation of

Christ will live in you as you open the door and invite him in.
EPHESIANS 3:17

G raduations, birthday parties, weddings, housewarmings. We get invited to be part of memorable occasions for the people we love.

One family wedding I will never forget took place in a sweet little cottage on a lake. It was a simple ceremony, but my anxiety was extremely high—because on this side of our family, I am a stepmom and step-grandma. Even though there is a lot of love to go around, our families don't see each other very often. Sometimes, I am not sure how I fit in when these important events take place. So I waited in the foyer with the men while the rest of the women in the family were in the bridal room.

Unexpectedly, a deeper invitation came. "Susie, come back with me to see the beautiful bride!" These generous moms and sisters I am step-related to welcomed me back to the bridal room. What a gift to spend time with this precious young woman I love before she walked down the aisle.

Everything about that day became different, more meaningful because of a personal invitation.

Being *invited* can change things.

Inviting someone can change things too.

Jesus does both. He *invites* us to participate in the abundant, grace-filled life that he offers us every single moment. And he waits to *be invited* into our lives. If we will ask him to be more present, part of what is going on, he will.

I love the image of Jesus standing at the door and knocking, waiting for the invitation to come in (see Revelation 3:20). But opening the door—inviting Jesus in—involves both risk and reward.

The risk? You must be willing to let him have *access*. You must give him permission to exercise *his* power in your life.

The reward? "Christ will live in you" (Ephesians 3:17). His help, love, peace, power, creativity, and joy can live in you. Is there anything you could possibly want more?

INVITE HIM IN

Ask Jesus into every good, bad, and unknown part of this day. Extend him a personal invitation into the deeper places inside of you. Go ahead and open that door. Every day of your life is a special occasion to him, and he wants to come in and make all the difference.

PRAYER

Dear Jesus, please make yourself at home in my heart. You are the only one I can trust with every single thing. Help me relinquish control and give you complete access to my needs. I *invite* you in right now.

YES

noun: an affirmative reply; a vote for
something; acceptance, agreement

*This is what we preach and pray, the great Amen, God's
Yes and our Yes together, gloriously evident. God affirms us,
making us a sure thing in Christ, putting his Yes within us.*
2 Corinthians 1:20-21

Yes. It's a mostly positive word. The answer "yes" can inspire celebration, new beginnings, smiles of relief.

I picture Jesus (and all of heaven) celebrating like crazy every time someone comes to him believing in his power to save and redeem them. Every time someone says yes to him.

When I said yes to Jesus, I remember feeling so excited, so ready. Yet at the same time, I was hesitant and a bit scared—wondering what I was getting myself into. This combination of emotions reminded me of swimming lessons as a kid. I loved them so much. I couldn't wait until "free time" when the high diving board would be open. It was probably only ten feet high, but in my six-year-old mind, it was a hundred feet up at least. I would hold my breath as my bare feet pressed into the wet, sandpapery surface of the diving board. Each step closer to the edge caused the board (and me) to waver more and more. But the exhilaration of flying into the air, the warmth and fun of splashing into the water, and the sense of strength and confidence that came with each jump kept me climbing that ladder over and over again.

Jumping off the high dive turned out to be my favorite thing about learning how to swim. And saying yes to Jesus has been my favorite thing about being in a relationship with him. It is so worth it to take the leaps of faith that he leads us to. The more we say yes to him, the more we discover all the ways he loves us, and the more we experience his goodness in our lives.

I try to remember this when it feels scary. When the diving board seems so high that I can't even see the water below. I start to convince myself that I am pretty comfortable right where I am...

But Jesus is waiting in the pool, and I know I can always trust him to catch me.

INVITE HIM IN

Go ahead and jump into God's *yes*. He has so many wonderful things prepared for you. You don't have to be afraid of what he has in mind. Because the most reassuring thing about saying yes to God is that he has already said yes to you. You can be confident and rest in the knowledge that you are affirmed by him. You have his "yes" vote, his acceptance for the rest of your life.

PRAYER

Dear Jesus, thank you that I can say *yes* to you, knowing that you have good in mind for me. I will jump into your arms, trusting with all my heart that you will be there.

Part Six

God's Tender Heart

ROOMY

adjective: having plenty of room; spacious

So spacious is [Jesus], so roomy, that everything of God finds its proper place in him without crowding.
COLOSSIANS 1:19

Do you ever wonder as you walk through a crowded mall or along a busy street how God could possibly know and love every individual on this planet? Not to mention every person of the generations upon generations before this one?

I start to think it's too much for him—that maybe he doesn't really have the capacity to keep track of all of us. Maybe just the neediest ones get his attention—oh, and probably the pastors and missionaries and Christian artists who sing and speak on stage for him.

But what about us? What about the ones who go to school, work, church (or not), and just try to find him in our regular lives? Don't we all blend in together? How could he possibly make space for us all?

God is roomy. Spacious. He has *plenty* of room. Maybe I need a bigger picture of who he is, like a huge floor plan of his heart or something. Maybe our roomy God has enough square footage for every single person in his family. Room enough to rest, to play, to grow. A safe place to be protected and cared for.

Room to be loved—no matter how messy we are.

As hard as it is to imagine, God is fully able to be with each and every one of us at the same time. That's the kind of heart our God has for us. A heart with space for all of us. A heart where we can each have our own room.

INVITE HIM IN

Ask our Father to show you *your* room—the space he has made just for you. Make this your retreat, your hiding place where you can be with him and be completely yourself. You don't have to wait for your turn to be heard. He is there waiting to spend time with *you*.

PRAYER

Dear Jesus, thank you that you have plenty of time, plenty of *room* for me. Please draw me close as I retreat to the quiet place you have created just for me in your heart. I will relax and be myself with you, knowing that you delight in the time we spend together.

UNTYING

verb: to free from something that ties, fastens, or restrains;
to disengage the knotted parts of something, resolve

He was never without a story when he spoke. When he
was alone with his disciples, he went over everything,
sorting out the tangles, untying the knots.
MARK 4:34

Untying something can be difficult. The longer a knot has existed, the harder it is to undo. I kind of like the challenge. Give me any shoe with a week-old, kid-tightened shoelace knot, and I will work it loose relentlessly. The smiles of relief and surprise are worth the sacrifice of time and messed-up fingernails.

But the real expert on untying is Jesus.

In this verse, he is not untying shoelaces; he is untying truth. He is explaining the meaning of his stories, helping his disciples understand God's message of love and reconciliation.

And Jesus is the one who can untie *our* knots and bring us clarity, freedom, and joy.

We all have questions about God and the Bible that we can't resolve on our own. Some of us have been hurt or disappointed by churches and religious people. Jesus brings *clarity* here. His message of love isn't supposed to be complicated or judgmental. Sometimes we humans mess that up. But he never does. He can untangle the emotions, the bitterness, the confusion, and help us understand the truth.

He brings *freedom* too. Many of us are bound by calendars and schedules that don't even allow us to breathe sometimes. He offers to help us rest in the middle of the overwhelming week or day when there's too much to do and not enough time. He whispers encouragement and fills us with strength that we can't muster up on our own. He quiets us with his constant presence, breathing peace and relaxing our spirits when we look to him.

And Jesus brings *joy*. As we take his promises to heart, we can surrender our fears and doubts to him. We can trust him to heal us within and restore our strained relationship with him. We can find hope even in the most difficult times. We can be absolutely sure that he is in control and will never leave us. We can celebrate as he replaces our fears with overwhelming joy.

INVITE HIM IN

Can you relax and let Jesus untie you? He wants to free you from your confusion, your stress, and your fear. He knows everything that binds your heart and mind, and he will patiently work out the knots. He loves you so much. Let him surprise you with the relief and joy that comes from trusting him.

PRAYER

Dear Jesus, I bring my knotted-up parts to you today. Help me humbly and gratefully receive your clarity, your freedom, your joy. Thank you that you are the master of *untying*.

Tend

verb: to apply oneself to the care of: to
watch over; to stand by in readiness

We're his people, his well-tended sheep.
PSALM 100:3

Tend. Such an old-fashioned word. I imagine people in simpler times tending the garden, tending the stove, tending the home. These things require more patience and focus than I have most of the time. And tending sheep? That sounds extraordinarily boring. What do shepherds even do anyway? Just sit and look at their sheep all day?

I started thinking that there must be something significant about the job of a shepherd, though, because Jesus sure talks about it a lot. After just a few minutes of searching online, I developed a new appreciation for this grueling occupation. Shepherds are expected to lead hundreds of sheep to water, food, and rest several times a day. Care for the sick and injured ones by delicately rubbing oil in their wounds to prevent disease. Hold them close to provide comfort and relief from their pain. "Like a shepherd, he will care for his flock, gathering the lambs in his arms, hugging them as he carries them" (Isaiah 40:11).

A shepherd must navigate dangerous pathways, keep every sheep from getting lost or left behind. He needs to stay alert and awake all day (and sometimes all night) to protect the sheep from predators. A truly dedicated shepherd will be prepared to give his own life to save the sheep from harm.

> David said, "I've been a shepherd, tending sheep for my
> father. Whenever a lion or bear came and took a lamb

from the flock, I'd go after it, knock it down, and rescue
the lamb. If it turned on me, I'd grab it by the throat,
wring its neck, and kill it" (1 Samuel 17:34-35).

Yikes.

Leading, caring, comforting, holding, navigating, keeping, staying, protecting, sacrificing...not to mention the terrible schedule
and harsh working conditions. What an overwhelming, demand-
ing, stress-filled job. I feel bad for making fun of it.

A shepherd has to be tender and tough at the same time.

Jesus is perfectly both. And we are the sheep who desperately
need him to be both for us.

INVITE HIM IN

Let him tend to you today. Come to him for all the things you
need: his leading, his healing, his comfort, his protection. You can
count on him to keep you from getting lost or left behind. Ask him
to stay with you for a while. He's already sacrificed his own life to
save you, proving his dedication and love. You can trust him to take
care of you day and night.

PRAYER

Dear Jesus, thank you that you are both tough enough and tender enough to take care of me. No matter what kind of trouble I get
myself into, I know that you are watching out for me always. Please
help me stay close to you as you guide me along my path today, *tending* my heart.

BREAKFAST

noun: a meal eaten in the morning, the first of the day

Jesus said, "Breakfast is ready."
JOHN 21:12

Breakfast. Some of us look forward to a steaming hot meal of eggs, bacon, and pancakes. Others grab a protein bar or a smoothie on the run. And lots of us skip it altogether. What we eat (or not) for breakfast isn't really the important thing to Jesus.

So why breakfast? Why is this meal important enough to be mentioned in John's Gospel? Why did Jesus make breakfast for his friends on the beach this particular morning?

I love to picture it. Jesus gathering wood for a fire, setting out plates, preparing the bread. Every so often, he might look out at the boat on the water and smile. He loved these guys, and he missed them. It had been several days since he had been crucified, and he knew they were struggling without him.

Not only had they been overwhelmed with grief and despair, but they were having a horrible time fishing. They had been up all night and caught nothing. They were discouraged that the job they had always known how to do wasn't going well. They were frustrated, exhausted, and probably really hungry.

And Jesus knew exactly what to do. When his friends were perhaps ready to give up and head in to shore, he surprised them with a net full of fish. At that moment, they were filled with joy—not so much because of the number of fish, but because they suddenly recognized Jesus. They rushed to him, and he took care of them, reviving their bodies with food and the warmth of the fire.

I like to think that he does this for us too. He knows when we are experiencing an awful time, when everything is going horribly wrong. He sees us: depressed, angry, hurting, and wondering why everything is happening to us all at once.

So he shows up. And he makes breakfast. Maybe not *literally*, but he really does have his eye on us, and he's always doing something good. He's on the beach, in the traffic, on the barstool, in the waiting room—just waiting to show us how much he cares. He is always welcoming us to come and sit by the fire with him and be restored.

INVITE HIM IN

Are you looking down, focusing on all the disappointments and frustrations around you? Look up. Recognize Jesus. Let him make you breakfast today. Sit with him for a minute and let him care for you, provide for you, and warm your heart. This meal, this conversation with Jesus...it might just turn your life around.

PRAYER

Dear Jesus, you are such a generous, loyal friend. You care deeply about my disappointments; you understand my discouragement; and you want to surprise me with something like *breakfast*. Thank you for taking care of me today.

NAME

noun: a word or combination of words by which a
person is known, addressed, or referred to

*Jesus took one look up and said, "You're John's son, Simon? From
now on your name is Cephas" (or Peter, which means "Rock").*
JOHN 1:42

Susan is the name on my birth certificate, my driver's license, my
credit card. But I don't really feel like a "Susan." Ever since I was a
baby, I have been called Susie by everyone I know. Susie just seems
to fit me. Apparently, the name Susie means "graceful lily,"[10] which
is kind of funny, since lilies are some of my least favorite flowers, and
I am far from graceful. (I think I might have failed ballet class. And
gymnastics.)

Our name is often the first thing people learn about us. Names
connect us to our family, our spouse, our culture, our sense of self. We
get attached to our names, and changing them can be complicated.

In the verse above, Simon (Peter) was being introduced to Jesus
by his brother Andrew. Since this was their initial meeting, it seems
a bit surprising to me that the first words Jesus said to Simon were
something like, "Hi. Good to meet you. Oh, by the way, I'm changing your name."

Why?

As far as we know, Jesus let all the other disciples keep their original names. It wasn't like part of the requirement for becoming a disciple involved a name change. But here goes Jesus again being gracious
and surprising with a bit of humor tucked inside his actions.

Jesus already knew Peter. He knew his personality, his gifts, his potential. He gave this impulsive, emotional, overeager fisherman a name that means "rock." I like to think that in giving him a new name right away, Jesus was giving Peter confidence, encouragement, and inspiration...a glimpse of God's glory before Peter could see it in himself. He knew that Peter was going to become one of the most influential leaders of the early church, boldly teaching about Jesus, firm in his faith. He saw this long before Peter could even imagine it. And he would remind him of what he saw in him every time he called his name.

INVITE HIM IN

Ask Jesus how he sees you. Ask him what he wants to do in and through you. You don't have to change your name. Jesus just wants to give you the confidence, the encouragement, and the inspiration to become the person he created you to be. He knows you completely right now, and he knows your potential—no matter what your name is or what it means. Let him give you a glimpse of glory today as he calls you by name.

PRAYER

Dear Jesus, thank you that you know me by much more than my *name*. You love me just the way I am, and you see me as you created me to be. Please help me live my life in a way that brings glory to *you*.

JOY

noun: a feeling or state of well-being and contentment; delight

Immersed in tears, yet always filled with deep joy.
2 CORINTHIANS 6:10

What makes you happy? What makes you smile? It's fun to think about those things. Success, relief, good news—all of these come wrapped up in happiness. Happiness just feels good.

But what about the days when we don't feel happy? When sadness overwhelms, the answer is *no*, the results are not good. When depression and discouragement weigh heavy on our hearts and we aren't even sure why. In the midst of disappointment, heartbreak, or loss, how can we possibly experience *joy*?

Jesus offers us something that reaches deeper and lasts much longer than that happy feeling. He wants to give us real joy: contentment, well-being, heartwarming hope, and a deep breath of peace. Even when things aren't going well. Even when our circumstances are awful.

Hope? There is so much more than we can see right now. Sometimes I have to remind myself that this life is not all there is. Jesus is the only one who sees the big picture and knows the whole story. He can bring beauty from ashes, good from evil, life from death.

Peace? Jesus is right here with us. He can walk us through to the other side of whatever we are experiencing. And if we will look to him with open hearts and hands, he will surprise us with so much good along the way.

The joy he has for us transcends the deepest pain. It holds us steady and keeps us smiling in our hearts, even when our eyes are filled with tears.

INVITE HIM IN

Open your heart—even just a crack. See if you can allow his joy to soothe where it hurts, calm your fears, and give you a glimpse of all that he has in store for you. It's okay to smile. Or not. He's got you either way. Let him fill you with the deep joy that only he can give.

PRAYER

Dear Jesus, thank you for the deep and lasting *joy* that comes from knowing you. Please help me feel encouraged and strengthened, even in my saddest and most painful times. I will look to you through tear-filled eyes and find real hope and peace.

CLEARLY

adverb: allowing easy and accurate perception, without doubt

We don't yet see things clearly.
1 CORINTHIANS 13:12

I have a love-hate relationship with eyeglasses. I love that someone invented lenses that can help us see things in focus. I hate that I need them—and can never find them when I need them.

Glasses are prescribed specifically to correct the vision of the person wearing them. If we look through lenses that were not designed for us, we won't be able to see very well at all. We do it all the time, though. We look through different lenses depending on how we feel and what we think.

Sometimes, when we are struggling with depression or fear, there is a cloudiness, a bluish-gray haze to everything we see. Sometimes we put on rose-colored or polarized lenses in order to justify our beliefs. And sometimes we just wear our reading glasses too long. We look only at what is right in front of us and forget to look up and see the bigger picture.

Much of the time, our glasses are smudged or foggy. Especially when we look at ourselves.

Jesus sees us so clearly, so perfectly. It must make him sad when he sees us looking at ourselves with criticism, finding fault and focusing so much on the dirty, cracked places.

But it's just so natural for me to notice the smudges and spots first. And sometimes I just can't see past them. Those mistakes I made? The things I don't do that I should? Those bad habits I can't break? The flaws in my appearance, my performance, my words?

They block my view. They keep me from seeing clearly, the way that Jesus sees me...

Covered in grace

Righteous, pure, forgiven

A new creation, his handiwork

Loved, chosen, treasured

Victorious, redeemed, light and salt for the world

His precious child and chosen friend

Oh Jesus, can you help us see ourselves the way you see us? Thank you for the hope in the last part of today's verse: "We'll see it all then, see it all as clearly as God sees us, knowing him directly just as he knows us!"

Invite Him In

Ask Jesus to help you see yourself the way he sees you. Let him show you the lenses of light and love that he views you through. Open your eyes to the bigger picture. Look up, look into his eyes, and let yourself trust him. He will clean your glasses for you every time you ask him to.

Prayer

Dear Jesus, please help me see with your eyes. I want to understand more *clearly* how you love me, how you love everyone. Thank you that one day I will know you better, just as you know me so well now.

HELP

noun: aid, assistance, remedy, relief

*It's exactly the same no matter what a person's religious
background may be: the same God for all of us, acting the
same incredibly generous way to everyone who calls out
for help. "Everyone who calls 'Help, God!' gets help."*
ROMANS 10:12-13

L ife can be such a struggle sometimes. We get lost, sick, distracted,
and overwhelmed. We try to handle things on our own, but sometimes we just can't. We need help. We need other people, and we
need Jesus. And God is so generous with both.

He loves to bring people into our lives who speak truth to us,
believe in us, inspire and encourage us. He knows our strengths and
weaknesses, and he matches them up with the strengths and weaknesses of others. No matter how capable or smart we are, there are
times we need to ask for help from the people in our world.

And we also need to ask for help from Jesus. He is our provider,
the only one who can give us everything we need: physical needs like
money for food and medical expenses, emotional needs like love and
acceptance, spiritual needs like forgiveness and freedom and close-
ness to him.

We are not alone. There are hundreds of stories and verses in
God's Word about the help he gives to his people. He understands
our human struggles, and he knows exactly what we need. He *wants*
to help us.

Sometimes he gives us guidance, comfort, encouragement
through a friend or even a stranger. Sometimes he changes a situation

by opening up a different opportunity, making a way, healing or restoring something broken. And sometimes he just wraps his arms around us through a terrible storm and holds us close.

INVITE HIM IN

Run to his welcoming arms of safety, comfort, and relief. Reach out to the people he has placed in your life. Whisper his name for guidance and support and peace. His heart of love will generously give you everything and everyone you need.

PRAYER

Dear Jesus, thank you for your *help*. You protect me, take care of me, and come close. I will depend on you no matter what kind of trouble comes my way.

SAND

noun: a loose granular substance formed from the erosion of
rocks; a major constituent of beaches, riverbeds, and deserts

Your thoughts—how rare, how beautiful!
God, I'll never comprehend them!
I couldn't even begin to count them—
any more than I could count the sand of the sea.
PSALM 139:17-18

My absolute favorite place is the beach. Any beach. A tropical beach with white sand and brilliant turquoise water. A rugged coastal beach with long stretches of golden sand and huge, deep blue waves crashing in. The familiar rocky beaches of the Puget Sound with grayish sand, seaweed ribbons, and calmer waters, all punctuated by seagull calls.

When it's warm enough, I take off my shoes and walk barefoot. I love the sand. It feels strangely comforting as it cushions my steps and works its way in between my toes. And it makes me think of Jesus.

It takes my heart to Psalm 139, which is all about how God made us, knows us, and thinks about us every moment. His thoughts are unique and intricate as he creates us, merciful when we make mistakes and struggle, protective and encompassing when we are in danger, full of grace and good for every moment of our lives. They are so generous, so numerous that we couldn't possibly count them.

Like the number of sand grains in the sea.

Incomprehensible. Immeasurable. Overwhelming.

I read about someone who tried to count sand. She spilled a

quarter teaspoonful onto a plate and began to separate the grains using a magnifying glass, a bright light, and a toothpick. After counting 100 in just 1 square centimeter of the pile, she roughly estimated the rest of the quarter teaspoon to hold approximately 10,000 grains of sand.[11]

Ten thousand grains of sand. In one *quarter of a teaspoon*. I start to wonder how many teaspoons of sand there are in the world...

God's thoughts. We don't have to count them. We just get to be grateful and reassured that he is always thinking about us. We are the recipients of his devoted attention, his deepest consideration, his constant care.

Invite Him In

Picture your favorite beach. Sit there with Jesus for a few minutes. Let the imaginary sand run through your fingers as you think about how much you mean to him. He has been thinking about you since before you were even born. He is thinking about you right this second. And he will continue to think about you every moment for the rest of your life. Go ahead—take off your shoes and get a little sand between your toes. It will remind you now (and when you find it later) that he loves you more than you could ever imagine.

Prayer

Dear Jesus, your thoughts, your ways number more than all the stars and grains of *sand* you created. It is humbling and amazing to me that I am on your mind every moment. Please help me live in the truth that your precious thoughts include me.

WEAR

verb: to habitually have on one's body as clothing, decoration, protection; to be dressed in

Regardless of what else you put on, wear love. It's your basic, all-purpose garment. Never be without it.
Colossians 3:14

We all have our go-to sweats. Or jeans. Or T-shirt. Worn and faded and stretched and soft.

I have my favorite old blue fleece that I have worn almost every day since I bought it in 1999. It's in pretty bad shape. But I just love everything about it. The fit, the weight, the color, the pockets, the embroidered Young Life logo on the side. I put it on almost every day when I get home. It feels especially good when I'm tired, sick, or cold.

In today's verse, we're being encouraged to wear *love*. My first thought when I read this verse was that we should try to look good, dress up, be fancy. But the more I thought about it, the more I realized that love should probably be our "go-to" outfit. Love should be our most comfortable, most familiar, easiest-to-throw-on thing. Something we want to wear every day, even when we don't feel good (or loving). Especially then. We don't have to impress, we just need to love—ourselves, our people, our Jesus.

If love is our "basic, all-purpose garment," we can show patience, kindness, understanding, and generosity from an authentic, comfortable place. We can feel secure enough in the love of Jesus that we can share it all day long.

His love is so available, so comforting, so essential. Let's live in it.

INVITE HIM IN

Ask Jesus to help you put on love today. Imagine his kindness warming you, cooling you, helping you relax. He's not worried about fashion. His concern is for his people. He wants us to experience his love so we can show it to each other, to everyone in our lives. He doesn't want anyone to be without it.

PRAYER

Dear Jesus, thank you for your abundance of love for me and everyone in my life. Please help me live in it today and every day. I want to *wear* love well.

FORGET

verb: to fail to remember something; to stop thinking
or caring about someone; neglect, disregard

*I'd never forget you—never. Look, I've written
your names on the backs of my hands.*
ISAIAH 49:15-16

Forgetting things. Forgetting people. It feels awful, doesn't it? We use all kinds of tricks and tips to remind us not to forget. We set alarms on our phones. We stick Post-it notes everywhere. We write on our hands or wear something that will help us remember. A friend of mine crosses her fingers at work until she gets back to her computer so she won't forget to send an important email. Forgetting makes us embarrassed, inconvenienced, and sometimes absolutely panicked.

And being the one forgotten? It can break your heart.

In Isaiah 49:14, the people of Jerusalem were crying out to God. Their city had been attacked and their temple destroyed by the Babylonians. *But Zion said, "I don't get it. GOD has left me. My Master has forgotten I even exist."* They felt like God had abandoned them.

God reassured them by saying that he would never forget them. Even if a mother could forget her child, God would never forget his precious people (verse 15). He comforted them, revealing to them that he has written their names on his hands.

And he has our names permanently engraved on his hands too. Your name. My name. Like a significant tattoo that represents what he values. Not because he is worried that he might forget us. He couldn't if he tried. We are part of him, chosen by him, always on his mind and in his heart.

What reassurance, what confidence we can have when we remember that God designed us! He knows us. Our names are what he chose to have written on his mighty, gentle hands that hold the whole world.

No matter how alone we feel or how disappointing life gets, we are never forgotten by our God.

INVITE HIM IN

Imagine Jesus writing your name. Lovingly, carefully on his hand, where he can always see it. He never stops thinking about you, watching over you, taking care of you. You are always in (and on) his hands.

PRAYER

Dear Jesus, thank you for your strong and gentle hands that hold the whole world. What incredible grace that you have written my name on them! Thank you that I matter so much to you that you will never *forget* me.

SEE

verb: to perceive by the eye; to recognize; to notice

You're the God who sees me!
GENESIS 16:13

I used to be afraid of bugs. I would squish them without a second thought. Please don't tell my kindergartners. After all, our little school is centered around an insect theme. Now I'm starting to appreciate all the fascinating details about insects and their critical roles on our planet. Learning about insects makes me even more in awe of our creative God.

We learned about the fairyfly the other day—the smallest known insect in the world.[12] One thousand four hundred different species of these wasps with tiny bodies and delicate wings have been discovered so far. Each one smaller than the period at the end of this sentence.

Almost invisible.

But not insignificant. Their short life span (likely only a few days) is vital to the health of critical crops like grapes, blackberries, and sugarcane. We need them.

Sometimes we feel as small as these creatures too. Insignificant. Almost invisible. We feel like we don't matter to anyone. We wonder if anyone cares.

I imagine that Hagar felt exactly like that. She had slept with the husband of her mistress, Sarai, in order to give Abram his first son. Her complicated situation had turned into a desperate one. She was alone in the desert, probably terrified, hopeless, and ashamed.

But God saw her. He had his eye on her the whole time. He knew exactly who she was and what she was going through. He visited her. He rescued her. He brought her favor, promise, hope.

Many of us can relate to Hagar. Much of the time we feel like outsiders, like the ones who never get recognized, like the ones who messed things up.

But the same God who saw Hagar's desperate heart sees our hearts. The same God who knew Hagar's story knows our stories. The same God who rescued Hagar and gave her a future rescues us. He visits us with his favor, his promise, his hope. He watches over us. He notices us. He sees us and loves us. Right where we are.

INVITE HIM IN

Allow Jesus to find you, to visit you. He already knows exactly where you are anyway. Let the amazing God who created 1,400 kinds of fairyflies take care of you. His is the God who watches over you, the God who rescues you, the God who has a beautiful purpose and future for you. Let him show you how he sees you through his eyes of love today.

PRAYER

Dear Jesus, thank you that you have your eyes of love on me. No matter how insignificant I feel or how badly I have messed up, you care deeply about me. Please help me remember that you are the one who truly *sees* my heart.

PART SEVEN

GOD'S CREATIVITY

WILD

adjective: uncontrolled, unruly; passionately eager
or enthusiastic; going beyond normal bounds

*Live full lives, full in the fullness of God. God can do
anything, you know—far more than you could ever
imagine or guess or request in your wildest dreams!*
EPHESIANS 3:19-20

The word *wild* scares me a little bit. Does it scare you? Wild animals, wild drivers, wild seas... In the presence of these wild things, I feel out of control and vulnerable. Give me a seat belt and life vest, please! I like safe.

Uncontrolled and *unruly*—these words unsettle my soul.

But what about the other parts of the definition?

"Passionately eager"? "Going beyond normal bounds"? How exciting to realize that God loves us that way. The fascinating kind of *wild*—far beyond anything we've ever imagined. This love of our God is wilder in its scope, its strength, its passion than we have ever dared to believe.

But it's still a little bit scary. Being loved by a wild God whom we don't completely understand and can't control.

Maybe we need his love to be wildly strong enough to hold us when we feel like we are spinning out of control. Maybe we need his love to reach beyond our wildest fears to save us from dangers real and imagined. And just maybe our "wildest dreams" are nothing compared to what God has in mind for us.

Can we let him love us like this? This God of ours who can do anything?

Our simple minds cannot comprehend this kind of love, but he can breathe it into our hearts and souls today.

INVITE HIM IN

Whether you need a strong gust of God's "passionately eager," enthusiastic love or just a reassuring whisper, he knows. Let's be brave and trust him to take us on the ride of our lives...lives of fullness in him. This God who loves us wildly has big plans for us if we will simply trust him. Take off your spiritual life vest and seat belt and hold his hand. Following him can be scary *and* safe at the same time.

PRAYER

Dear Jesus, thank you for being a *wildly* creative, passionately loving God. I want to be swept up in all the fullness and excitement of this life with you. Please help me to expand my limits and let you take control.

WONDER

verb: to desire to know; to be curious about;
to be astonished, amazed, surprised

Your eye is a lamp, lighting up your whole body. If you live wide-eyed in wonder and belief, your body fills up with light.
LUKE 11:34

One of my favorite things about teaching kindergartners is the sense of wonder they bring to school. They are so curious, so imaginative, so full of questions. They make me want to wonder a bit more, to open my eyes a whole lot wider. It's contagious. And joyful.

God made us innately curious, but sometimes we forget to be. We explain things away or give them very little thought. We get used to things the way they are. Comfortable. Bored. Blah.

Maybe we can remember what it feels like to be five years old again. Maybe our whole world would light up if we would just get curious about Jesus. What if we wonder a bit more about God's tender love for his children? Would our hearts fill up? Would we snuggle a little closer to our Father, who holds us and heals us?

What if we stop for a minute to admire his stunningly beautiful creation? The thunderous power of his winds and waves and mountains? The intricate details of a snowflake, a rosebush, a firefly? The enormity of the universe and the brilliance of the stars? Would our faith grow bigger? Would we start to believe that he can do anything?

What if we pay more attention to the ways that God connects us to each other? Would we start to realize that he is the mutual friend of all his children? That he delights in bringing people into our lives at just the right time? Would we be able to see more clearly how he works in our everyday stuff, through imperfect people, to bring good and light?

And what if we started imagining more about what it is going to be like when he comes back for us? About heaven?

I wonder what Jesus and I will talk about as we look back on my life. My questions answered, his mysteries revealed. Love and grace and redemption woven throughout my story.

Makes me teary.

Makes me wonder if there is so much more that he would like to show me, show *us*, while we're still here…

INVITE HIM IN

Open your eyes wide to Jesus. Ask him to show up in astonishing and amazing ways. His creative power, his heart for connection, his plans—let him work them all together for good in your day-to-day life. He will light up your whole world and make it *wonderful*.

PRAYER

Dear Jesus, please help me be a child in your presence for a little while. I want to look at who you are and what you are doing with a new sense of *wonder*. Thank you that you will light up my life in a million new ways when I open my eyes to you.

MORE

noun: a greater quantity, number, or
amount; something additional

*Now that you've found you don't have to listen to sin tell you
what to do, and have discovered the delight of listening to God
telling you, what a surprise! A whole, healed, put-together
life right now, with more and more of life on the way!*
ROMANS 6:22

My friend's sweet baby boy just learned the sign for *more* in American Sign Language. He puts his cute little fingers together for more bottle, more peaches, more cereal. It is melt-your-heart adorable. Pretty much makes me want to give him everything.

We all want more, don't we? More sleep, more money, more time, more recognition. Maybe we were created with this strong desire for *more* so we would keep searching until we find more of Jesus.

He desires to give us:

more peace

more healing

more love

more freedom

more grace

more life

In the Bible, Jesus often surprises people with *more*. Over and over, I am amazed by how completely he understands, how deeply he cares, how big he thinks. One of my favorites is the story of the Samaritan woman at the well in John 4. Jesus surprises her completely by talking to her in the first place. Then he surprises her by knowing her whole story and offering her "living water" (verse 10). In that one unexpected conversation (as this woman is basically running errands), Jesus fills her heart and changes her life.

He loves us like that. He loves us like I love my friend's baby asking for more water in his high chair. Jesus knows exactly what we need more of right at this moment, and he is excited to give it to us.

> There are so many other things Jesus did. If they were all written down, each of them, one by one, I can't imagine a world big enough to hold such a library of books (John 21:25).

This is how John ends his Gospel, by telling us that there is so much we don't know about Jesus yet. That there is so much *more* to find out about him.

INVITE HIM IN

Ask Jesus for more of him. He knows your story. He wants to give you the "whole, healed, put-together life" he has for you. Good gifts, meaningful relationships, surprises of love and peace and joy in an ordinary day. Instead of grasping and struggling, take a deep breath and open your hands to receive from him. He will give you everything you need...and more!

PRAYER

Dear Jesus, "more and more of life." More and more of you. That is what I'm seeking! Please surprise me, fill me, and show me *more* of what you want to do in my heart and my world.

COLORS

noun (plural): properties that become apparent
when light falls on an object; the appearance
of authenticity; shade, brilliance, glow

You're here to be light, bringing out the God-colors in the world.
MATTHEW 5:14

Sixty-four colors. When I was in elementary school, I thought all the colors in the world were in that Crayola box with the built-in sharpener in the back. I remember carefully pressing open the thin cardboard lid and taking it all in—the rows of perfectly lined tips, the waxy-fresh smell, the different shades of greens and blues and reds. It was so hard to decide which one to use first. I loved every color—especially magenta. But as huge as that box seemed back in my elementary school days, it wasn't really very big compared to today's boxes of 96 and more. Apparently, the biggest box the Crayola company currently produces offers 152 different colors of crayons.[13]

But God's box of crayons is the biggest one of all. There are literally millions of colors for us to see in this world he has created, and many more that our eyes can't even perceive yet. I was excited to learn that a new shade of blue had been accidentally discovered a few years ago by electronics scientists at Oregon State University. Crayola now has a new crayon color based on this discovery. Its name? "Bluetiful."[14] Can't wait to try it.

The creativity and purpose of color is evident in art, in nature, in science, in *us*. Colors have power. They make us feel. They inspire; they calm; they distinguish things one from another. They brighten;

they darken; they warm us up and cool us down. They attract; they repel; they bring joy...

So, what are "God-colors"?

What does he want to reveal to the world when he shines his light on us?

God desires to show his peace, his hope, his joy, and his grace through his people. And most of all, he wants to reveal his love. With all the millions of shades and hues, all the possible combinations and complements of our personalities, he wants us to color a beautiful picture of who he is. He wants us to reflect him in the most genuine, creative, compassionate ways. Let's decorate our world with the light of our colorful, creative God.

INVITE HIM IN

Jesus made you in his image and filled you with his light and love. Let him shine this brilliant light through you today. Watch as he reflects the radiant hues of his love to the people in your life. He might even reveal to you a brand-new color, uniquely yours. Go ahead and surprise the world with it!

PRAYER

Dear Jesus, thank you for every single *color* you have created. Thank you for being the true light that falls on your people, that reveals your character in so many beautiful, radiant ways. Please help me shine brightly and uniquely for you today.

CONTAINER

noun: an object that can be used to hold
something; vessel, receptacle, holder

*Become the kind of container God can use to present any
and every kind of gift to his guests for their blessing.*
2 TIMOTHY 2:21

I admit that I get really excited about storage. I can spend hours at Storables or Target, organizing in my mind the ideal pantry, closet, or desk drawer. Quite often, however, the containers I end up with cost more than whatever is going to be stored inside.

I love the idea that God wants us to be containers. I'm all in. Glass jars, woven baskets, plastic boxes with snappy lids, metal tubs, canvas bins... But by focusing on the containers so much, I might be missing the point. Maybe what's most important about storing things is not the container itself, but what's inside. What it holds.

We have the privilege of holding the Spirit of God inside us. He gives us the opportunity to be his vessels—ready to share "any and every kind of gift" with this world. Love, grace, understanding, support, relief, care, freedom...There are so many ways that we can "present" these gifts from God.

Maybe with such beautiful, valuable things inside us, we don't need to spend so much time thinking about our outward appearance. As cute as those pin-striped canvas bins and decorative canisters are, they are actually not the most effective.

When I really think about it, my go-to containers are the ones I can reach quickly and open easily. The ones that clearly show what's inside. The ones with plenty of room.

Can we be like this? Accessible to the ones who need us, ready to listen and help and give? Visible to those around us? Offering them something real and life-changing? Opening up space in our hearts for people we know and people we don't?

Does what the world see in us bring people closer to Jesus?

INVITE HIM IN

Ask Jesus to shine through you. He loves that you are his child, and he delights to live in your heart. As he continually fills you with his Spirit, his light and joy are revealed to everyone around you. Try not to worry about your "container." It's not nearly as valuable as what you hold inside.

PRAYER

Dear Jesus, thank you for placing your Spirit inside me. What a privilege to be your *container*—holding such a powerful, life-breathing gift! Please open up space in my heart and day to bless the people around me with your presence and love.

Detail

noun: a part considered separately from the whole; a
single piece of information; item, particular, point

Every detail in our lives of love for God is worked into something good.
Romans 8:28

Details are just not my thing. I like to imagine the finished project, the big picture, the happy ending. Working out the specifics, figuring out the step-by-step process is hard for me.

But God is so good at them. Oftentimes, it is in the details that we find his truth and hope.

Truth: God knows us better than we know ourselves. He created us for a purpose. He is familiar with every detail of our lives.

Hope: He is good. Even in the hurt and stress that we can't see our way out of, we are held in his strong and gentle hands.

Today's verse reminds us that God cares deeply about each one of us. He is putting something special together with all these parts of us that can seem so separate, so random, so confusing.

God is the creator of the universe, the most brilliant artist, the master of design. As we make our way through our days, our weeks, our years, he is painting, sculpting, or sketching something beautiful with our lives.

Or maybe he is weaving...

Perhaps for some of us, our experience with weaving consists of a toy: a small, plastic, spiky square and some elastic bands. Pot holders for everyone that Christmas! But Jesus is creating something much more valuable on his loom. He has our life stories in front of him, and every detail has an essential part in the finished product.

Our people? Scattered strands of soft denim and crunchy raffia.

Our accomplishments and celebrations? Thin strips of cool cotton and crisp linen.

Our heartaches, failures, and grief? Rich, warm, velvety threads of gold.

Our happiest memories, our favorite things? Brilliant splashes of colorful silk throughout.

And the finished product? The tapestry he will display in the halls of heaven? It will tell the intricate, redeeming story of his love for us, his work in us. All the details included, valued, woven together for good.

INVITE HIM IN

Hold on tight to this promise from Jesus of truth and hope. Ask him to show you a glimpse of his magnificent design for your life. You can trust that his finished product is going to be indescribably beautiful. He is taking care of all the details.

PRAYER

Dear Jesus, thank you that every part of my life matters to you. The tiniest of *details* are in your hands. Even when I don't understand how things can possibly work out, please help me trust that you are holding everything together, and you will bring good out of it.

DIFFERENT

adjective: not the same as another; unlike in
nature, form, or quality; distinct, separate

*How much different is it now as you live in God's freedom,
your lives healed and expansive in holiness?*
ROMANS 6:19

In getting to know my new teammates at work the other day, I shared
with them that I am a Christian. They nodded politely and smiled,
and we went on sharing about our interests and families.

I got to thinking about it later. What does it mean to someone when we say, "I'm a Christian"? I assume it means a variety of
things—good, bad, and ugly—depending on who we are talking to
and what experiences they have had with church and religion.

But what does it mean for *us*? How is life different? How are *we*
different because we belong to Jesus?

Do we have to dress a certain way, use specific words, or carry a
Bible around all the time? Nope. That's the beauty of belonging to
him. God made each of us distinctly his, and he doesn't expect us
to give up our personalities or quirks or styles. (Unless something is
harmful to you or others, of course. He'll help you work through it.)

What's *different* about us is that his Spirit is growing life-giving
fruit inside us. It's like he's got a huge orchard full of his children.
He plants his Spirit in our hearts when we invite him in, and growth
begins. Sometimes we can see the fruit right away, and sometimes it
grows over time. Fruit like...

Love: the unselfish kind that says encouraging things or
nothing at all

Joy: the deep kind that is present even when things are not "happy"

Peace: the underlying calm in the midst of stressful and overwhelming days

Grace: the willingness to listen, to empathize, to forgive

Faith: the certainty that God is good and hears us when we pray

The ways that this fruit becomes evident in our lives are as unique and creative as we are, but the commonality is that it's all from Jesus. That's what we want people to know. He lives inside us, and our lives are free, redeemed, new. Not perfect, not following a certain formula—just marked by a willingness to grow and share the fruit that comes from him.

I hope that when people see me, they will want some of this fruit. I hope they will want to be planted in his orchard too. Don't you?

INVITE HIM IN

Ask Jesus to make you extraordinarily, noticeably different for him. He can cultivate the most beautiful fruit you can ever imagine. It will grow in and out of you if you trust him. Let him share his love, joy, peace, grace, and faith with everyone in your life. Including you.

PRAYER

Dear Jesus, thank you that because of you, I am *different*. Life is different. Even death is different. Thank you for giving me a place to grow in the orchard of your love.

PART

noun: a piece or segment of something which, combined with other pieces, makes up the whole; function, role, component

A body isn't just a single part blown up into something huge. It's all the different-but-similar parts arranged and functioning together... God has carefully placed each part of the body right where he wanted it.
1 Corinthians 12:14,18

'm waiting for my car to be repaired. Again. I guess when you have a car that is 18 years old, this is what you get to do. Replace parts. Big parts or small ones, expensive or cheap, in stock or not. There are over 10,000 parts in the engine of a car, and it's important that they are all in working order.

Even the tiniest part matters. A spark plug, for example. Just a few inches in size, but its role is critical. In the same way, each individual believer is part of the body of Christ: God's incredible machine that works to bring him glory. His amazing design brings all of us into a relationship with him.

We each play a vital role in this engine. We all need to function so that the whole thing runs. We might be bigger, noticeable parts like pastors, missionaries, and conference leaders. Or we might have seemingly smaller roles like teaching Sunday school, writing notes of encouragement, or visiting nursing homes.

We need to remember that these abilities God gives us match up perfectly with the abilities he gives to others.

Complementing. Not comparing.

Cooperating. Not competing.

Unfortunately, most of us aren't exactly sure how to play our part, how to just do what God asks us to do without worrying about how we measure up. We constantly check ourselves against others, question our worth, try to do more than we are meant to. We often wish we could have a more significant part.

Let's remind ourselves that each of us is a necessary part of God's intricate design. Some of us are called to help, some to teach, some to encourage, some to lead, some to serve. God masterfully simplifies and separates our roles to bring everything back together. And he has placed us just exactly where he wants us.

INVITE HIM IN

Look to God. Trust his wisdom as he helps you understand your role in his incredible plan. He knows your strengths, your gifts, and he will connect you with people who *need you* and people whom *you need*. He is really good at putting things together. Every single part.

PRAYER

Dear Jesus, thank you that you are the one who so magnificently completes everything for your good. I trust you to give me everything I need to be effective for you. Please help me be faithful to the *part* you have chosen for me.

MYSTERY

noun: profound, inexplicable, or secretive quality or character

Christ, God's great mystery. All the richest treasures of
wisdom and knowledge are embedded in that mystery
and nowhere else. And we've been shown the mystery!
COLOSSIANS 2:2-3

Mysteries are intriguing, suspenseful, fun. We watch movies and read books about unsolved crimes, disappearances, conspiracies. The stories grab us and pull us in. The twists and turns keep us on the edge of our seats, and the solutions bring satisfaction and relief.

It's kind of a wild ride being a mystery buff. I started early. I read every single Nancy Drew book when I was young—all 64 of them. As soon as I finished one, I would start another. I would try to solve the mysteries myself, thinking ahead and predicting the solution. But I was almost always surprised by the ending, and I loved that too.

Mysteries make great stories, fiction or nonfiction. An unusual occurrence or puzzling series of events is eventually resolved by clever detective work. And maybe a bit of luck or chance, with several unexpected happenings along the way.

But God's great mystery is more than just a story. It is truth. It is his good news of grace in the person of Jesus Christ.

The accounts of Jesus's life on this earth are unusual, perplexing, unclear to some of us. So many things about his birth, his death, and everything in between are difficult to understand. Nobody could have predicted that this would be the way God would reveal himself to the world. And it is almost impossible to know what he is going to do next.

But we have been shown this mysterious Jesus. We continue to uncover truth—"the richest treasures of wisdom and knowledge"—as we get to know him better. And what's especially exciting is that God has made all of us important characters with him in this revelation.

We can be reassured that with God as the author, this mystery story has a wonderful ending. We can trust that he is going to wrap it all up for us, completing our understanding and answering our questions. Giving us relief after this wild ride we have been on.

And I'm pretty sure he is going to surprise us with the joy of the ending...

INVITE HIM IN

Thank Jesus for the mystery of knowing him. Ask him to make you more and more curious about him and how he loves you. Look for clues, listen for his voice, and expect him to show up in whatever you have going on today. Don't be afraid of the twists and turns. He will be right there with you every step of the way.

PRAYER

Dear Jesus, thank you for revealing yourself to me. I am humbled and grateful to know and be known by God's great *mystery*. Please help me not to keep you a secret, but to share the treasure that I have found in you.

Useless

adjective: not fulfilling the intended purpose
or desired outcome; ineffective, futile

Salt is excellent. But if the salt goes flat, it's useless, good for nothing.
LUKE 14:34-35

I almost bought a T-shirt the other day. It was black with a fun white font and the simple logo of one of my favorite coffee shops near a beach. It's a beautiful place with an unfortunate name: Useless Bay. I changed my mind about the T-shirt, though, when I thought about actually walking around with the word *useless* across my chest.

That is just a sad word. I'm not useless. You aren't useless. I don't think anyone would want to be described that way.

Jesus reminds us not to *become* useless—not that we would intentionally do that. But in the verse above, Jesus is preparing his disciples to go and bring people into his kingdom. He is using the analogy of salt and warning them that it has the potential to go flat. Salt that has lost its essential properties of cleansing and healing and preserving isn't really good for anything. Salt that has lost its flavor might as well be thrown away.

Jesus doesn't want his followers to get too attached to the things of this world so that we just blend in and become ineffective. He doesn't want us to lose our seasoning—the joy and hope of belonging to him that people notice.

So, what is Jesus really asking us to do? Should we wear T-shirts that say "useful" instead? I don't really like that word for describing people either.

He wants to use us, but not in an impersonal, manipulative way.

He wants to do his work in and through us—through our individual, creative, encouraging, honest, loyal, prayerful selves. He wants us to help bring people to him (or back to him) with love and truth. He wants us to hang in there with people, to not give up on anyone, even ourselves.

> My dear friends, if you know of people who have wandered off from God's truth, don't write them off. Go after them. Get them back and you will have rescued precious lives from destruction and prevented an epidemic of wandering away from God (James 5:19-20).

Let's be flavorful and effective as we show people our Jesus.

INVITE HIM IN

Ask God to give you a word for your T-shirt today. He won't give you *useless* (or *useful*), because he has a spicier name for you. Maybe you are a distinct kind of salt, like Himalayan pink or Hawaiian black lava or garlic? Maybe you are more of a cinnamon, licorice, or chili pepper spirit? What word, what creative logo would he put on your shirt? He gives you your flavor, and he will season this world with you if you let him!

PRAYER

Dear Jesus, thank you for giving me a purpose and a flavor. I don't want to ever become *useless*. Please make me effective for you— good and tasteful, spicy and strong.

Together

You were all called to travel on the same road and in the same direction, so stay together, both outwardly and inwardly.
Ephesians 4:4

I do it myself!" Any of us who have ever cared for a toddler have heard those words. In fact, we have probably all said them ourselves. When my boys were little, one of our favorite books was *All by Myself* by Mercer Mayer. The cute little animal character tries to do everything on his own—tying shoes, riding a bike, buttoning his overalls—every page illustrating the struggle for independence as well as the importance of accepting help.

We live in an extremely independent culture. We grow up thinking that we need to be self-sufficient and ultra-capable. We get the message that it is a sign of weakness to depend on anybody else or ask for help. And some of us take this to heart more than others. We try to "pull ourselves up by our bootstraps," even when our arms are broken.

Jesus didn't mean for us to work in isolation, to do everything on our own. Especially when it comes to following him.

> When two of you get together on anything at all on earth and make a prayer of it, my Father in heaven goes into action. And when two or three of you are together because of me, you can be sure that I'll be there (Matthew 18:19-20).

So, it's God's idea that we should pray with one another. And it's so meaningful, so important to him that he will be there with us!

> Let's see how inventive we can be in encouraging love
> and helping out, not avoiding worshiping together as
> some do but spurring each other on (Hebrews 10:24-25).

So, church is not supposed to be a "rush in and out" thing. Could it be that God designed church to be more of an intimate place of connecting with others—encouraging and being encouraged as we worship him?

> The goal is for all of them to become one heart and
> mind—just as you, Father, are in me and I in you, so they
> might be one heart and mind with us. Then the world
> might believe that you, in fact, sent me (John 17:21).

People are watching. They can see Jesus (or not) by how we live in community with one another. They notice when we help and when we *let ourselves be helped* by one another. And the example is powerful enough that it can draw someone in or turn them away.

I need to stop trying to do it "all by myself." Want to work together with me on this?

INVITE HIM IN

Ask him to show you your place in his community of believers. Maybe he wants to give you a friend to pray with, a welcoming church family, or a colleague to depend on. Let him lead you together.

PRAYER

Dear Jesus, thank you for calling me to be connected to others who love you. Please help us to find hope and strength as we join *together* in worship and service to you.

Part Eight

God's Redemption

RESCUE

verb: to save from danger or harm; to free from confinement

*I greet you with the great words, grace and peace! We know the
meaning of those words because Jesus Christ rescued us from
this evil world we're in by offering himself as a sacrifice for
our sins. God's plan is that we all experience that rescue.*
GALATIANS 1:3-4

The Finest Hours. Bridge of Spies. Hacksaw Ridge. All inspired by true
stories. I think I loved these movies because of the dramatic rescues
that took place in each one. The danger, the risk, the incredible courage that was shown. I cannot imagine being half as brave and unselfish as the characters in these films.

What would it feel like to be one of the rescued ones? One of the
desperate victims of a storm, war, or captivity—saved because someone believed you were worth it?

Wanted. Valued. Deeply cared for. Irreplaceable.

It is hard to believe anyone would willingly die so that I could
stay alive.

But the amazing truth is that we all have someone who did just
that for us. Jesus Christ. The Lamb of God. Our hero. He sacrificed
his life and rescued us. He came after us with everything he had,
knowing he would lose it all. He freed us from the prison of sin and
death and gave us life with him...grace and peace like we've never
known.

That must mean we are pretty important to Jesus.

Wanted. Valued. Cared about. Worth it.

What an incredible relief to be ransomed by him! What a wondrous gift to be part of this story of love and redemption and joy!

And it's the truest story we know.

INVITE HIM IN

Thank Jesus for the incredible story he is writing with your life. He knows exactly what confines you and the danger you are in. He sees the fear, the shame, and the doubt that keeps you locked up and desperate to be rescued. And he came to get you. He gave his life so that you can have yours right now—forgiven, safe, and free. Run into his arms of love!

PRAYER

Dear Jesus, thank you for giving your life to *rescue* me. Your sacrifice paid the price for all my sin and delivered me from the evil of this world. Please help me live in the freedom and joy that come from belonging to you.

RULES

noun (plural): a prescribed guide for
conduct or action; laws, regulations

*If a living relationship with God could come by
rule-keeping, then Christ died unnecessarily.*
GALATIANS 2:21

Kids must think that teachers just *love* rules. They probably imagine
us cackling with delight as we create lists to ruin their fun. But it's
actually difficult work to come up with rules that teach appropriate
behavior for school without overwhelming kids.

Especially on the playground. There's a lot to remember just to
play on the slide:

One person at a time.

Feet first.

Only travel *down* the slide—no climbing up.

Stay seated—no standing.

Whew. It's a lot to do things right every time. Sometimes kids
don't, so we keep working on it. What we try to help them understand is the *purpose* of the rules. We want everyone to have fun on
the slide and not get hurt.

For Christians, rules are extra complicated. We start with the
Ten Commandments, and then we add to them the expectations of
our family, our denominations, our teachers, ourselves. We have so
many dos and don'ts, we can't possibly keep track of them all, much
less follow them. We feel guilty a lot.

But maybe we are focusing way too much on the specifics and

missing the whole point. Maybe the purpose of the rules isn't to keep every single one and somehow think we are earning our way to Jesus.

Maybe the purpose of the law and message of Jesus is simply *love*.

He wants us to love him with all our heart, soul, mind, and strength and to love our neighbors (our family, our friends, the coffee barista, the driver in front of us, the challenging teenager or toddler, the negative coworker, etc.) as we love ourselves (see Mark 12:30-31).

We forget to *love*. The purpose of the rules gets lost in the keeping of the rules. It happens all the time. We judge ourselves and others; we decide what kind of Christian everybody is by how well they follow the rules. We forget that Jesus wants everyone to experience his joy and not get hurt.

The good news is that Jesus did *not* die unnecessarily. His death on the cross paved the way for the forgiveness of all our sin and rule breaking. Whether we are good at keeping rules or not, believing in him is the only way that we can have a right relationship with God.

INVITE HIM IN

Ask Jesus to help you stop trying to rule-follow your way to him. Step out of the rigidity and relax in his presence. He's already done the work of making you good and accepted and free. Let his grace and peace and joy fill you to overflowing so that you can't help but follow the most important rule of all: *love*.

PRAYER

Dear Jesus, no matter how hard I try, I can't keep all the *rules*. Because of your grace, I no longer have to in order to be holy and saved. Thank you that you sacrificed your life to make me right with you.

MISFIT

noun: a person who does not seem to belong
in a particular group or situation

Invite some people who never get invited out, the misfits from the
wrong side of the tracks. You'll be—and experience—a blessing.
LUKE 14:13-14

We all feel like misfits sometimes. There are groups of people and certain situations where we don't fit in. Or we fit poorly, and it's painfully obvious. Like trying to squeeze into shoes that are simply too small. It doesn't feel good. It's uncomfortable. It hurts.

I have felt like a misfit for a lot of my life.

Church? I'm probably not good enough to be involved here. If they only knew...

Sports? I love them, but I'm not very fast. Or strong. Or skilled.

Social groups? I get nervous. What if I say the wrong thing? What if I do something weird? What if they don't like me?

I have been on the other side of this word too. I have been comfortable in a group and given myself power to decide who fits and who doesn't. Not outwardly, but in my mind and heart. Judging people by my own measures, my own standards. Separating them based on my limited understanding and their outward appearances.

This doesn't feel right either. This is even *more* uncomfortable when I think about it. And it *really* hurts.

It hurts Jesus too. When he was walking on this earth, he looked out for the misfits, the ones cast out and alone. He went to them. He touched lepers, restored sight to the blind, and invited tax collectors to eat with him. For years, these people had been on the outside because of the shame and judgment attached to them.

But Jesus validated them. He gave them worth and belonging. He lifted them up in the eyes of the "in" crowd, and he lifted them up in their own eyes. He didn't just give them a charitable donation; he gave them friendship and time. He listened to them. These people who were never invited to anything were invited to come and be close to Jesus.

He blessed them, and he gave them a chance to be a blessing too. He asks us to do the same.

INVITE HIM IN

Jesus has his eyes on you. He's inviting you to be in his group of friends, and you absolutely belong. And when you feel comfortable in the middle of the "in" crowd, ask Jesus to take you to the edge— to show you the misfits in your world, the ones left out and lonely. He will put you with someone who needs a smile, an encouraging word, a friend. You will be blessings to each other. He will make a perfect fit.

PRAYER

Dear Jesus, thank you for welcoming a *misfit* like me into your crowd. Please help me show everyone in my world the love and dignity that you would show them. I want to be more like you.

PIECES

noun (plural): broken or irregular parts of something; fragments

*GOD made my life complete
when I placed all the pieces before him.*
PSALM 18:20

"C areful...don't break it!" How many times have you heard that in your life?

Of course you didn't want to break Grandma's Christmas platter or the preschool handprint made of clay. You didn't *try* to break the jar of salsa all over the floor...

Broken stuff is upsetting. And messy.

And it can hurt so much. Especially when the breaking happens inside. When it's a heart that is in pieces. But just because something is in pieces doesn't mean it's ruined. I like to think there is a lot of hope for broken things.

When 8-year-old Ty broke both bones in his right forearm, our basketball-loving, baseball-playing kid was devastated. But as soon as those fractured bones were in a cast up to his shoulder, healing began to take place. New bone cells grew, new connections were formed. A few weeks later, when 12-year-old Andy's wrist got slammed into the boards during a hockey game, he joined his brother in this process of breaking and healing and new growth. We had a double dose of it that winter.

Within months, though, arms had healed and casts came off. Growth and time had sealed together the broken pieces in new and healthy ways. Instead of just getting back to normal, their bones had actually become stronger than they were before.

Not only can broken things become stronger, they can become more beautiful. In Japan, mending broken pottery is an inspiring art form called *kintsugi*: "golden joinery."[15] Instead of throwing away the broken pieces of a vase or teacup, artists carefully seal them back together using a special lacquer sprinkled with expensive gold. The restored piece with its unique golden design is regarded as even more pleasing, more valuable than it was before. A treasure.

That's what Jesus wants to do with us. He wants to scoop up our broken pieces and put them back together in stronger and more beautiful ways. No matter how many cracks we have, Jesus can take our rough places, our sharp edges, our painful parts and create an amazing work of art. Unique. Valuable. Even better than before.

INVITE HIM IN

Jesus knows what broken feels like. That's what happened to him on the cross. His body, broken for you. His precious blood, shed for you. He became broken so you don't have to stay that way. Go ahead and give him all your pieces. Just place them in his nail-scarred hands and let him begin the new growth, the healing, the delicate bonding and painting. He will make you into a beautiful treasure, stronger than ever before.

PRAYER

Dear Jesus, you understand that the broken *pieces* of my heart hurt sometimes. Please help me give them to you, trusting you to heal and strengthen me. Thank you that you are so faithful to restore me when I am falling apart.

FINISH

noun: the quality or state of being perfected; finale

Saving is all his idea, and all his work. All we do is trust him
enough to let him do it. It's God's gift from start to finish!
EPHESIANS 2:8

The end. Sad words on the last page of a wonderful book. Or at the end of a really good movie. I just want them to last a little longer. But when it comes to projects around the house or yard, the end can't come fast enough. I am so impatient with the process. I want to fast-forward through it, get it done. Now.

Years ago, we had a house built on our property. It was a dream to watch the process proceed from magazine photos and sketches on paper to a painted, furnished, completed house. But it almost drove me crazy. Everything took longer than I had anticipated. *Everything.* I thought it would never be done.

But it wasn't my work. It wasn't up to me. I just had to watch and wait and be patient.

When we finally moved in, we knew for sure that it had been worth the wait. The annual Lighthouse Festival in our town was booming. As we looked out from our new balcony, we were surprised with the most fantastic fireworks show we had ever seen. And the finale? Indescribable, amazing, so joyful.

When it comes to the building of our character—our growth in Jesus—it's so important to let him be in charge of the pace. It's tempting to want to rush it along, speed through the painful stuff, skip the hardest parts altogether. But he doesn't let us do that.

Jesus walks us through our growing process with perfect wisdom and timing. He is the one in charge of the work, after all. When it feels painfully slow, he will hold us close and remind us that we are in his hands and he knows what he is doing. Some of our most important lessons take the longest.

"Saving is all his idea, and all his work," as today's verse reminds us.

It's not up to us. It is his *gift*. And the best part? We will get to enjoy the finished product. Life in him—new, perfect, beautiful life with him forever. We can trust him for a grand finale.

INVITE HIM IN

Whatever you are waiting for, struggling with, tired of—give it over to him. Again and again if you have to. Trust in his perfect timing, knowing that he will complete his work in you. He is wise and faithful, and he loves you so much. You can look forward to the end of your story with confidence and joy.

PRAYER

Dear Jesus, thank you for your grace that saves me. Thank you that this gift of salvation is not something I have to complete on my own. Please help me remember that you are in charge of *finishing* what you have begun in me.

CHARACTERS

noun (plural): individuals marked by
notable or conspicuous traits

*When Jesus was eating supper at Matthew's house with his
close followers, a lot of disreputable characters joined them.*
MATTHEW 9:10

We all know a few characters. We silently admire the entertaining ones, the outgoing ones, the individuals who live life a little differently than we do. But when the word *disreputable* is added, any admiration turns to scorn. We think of the dishonest, unethical, opportunistic, self-serving people who don't play by the same rules we do.

Jesus sought out these characters. He acknowledged people who had terrible reputations. He talked to those whom no one else would reach out to—sometimes even sharing a meal with them. It was infuriating to the religious people of his time. They could not understand why he would choose to spend his time with them.

One of those disrespected characters Jesus paid attention to was Matthew, a tax collector, likely despised by most people. In a move that would have shocked everyone, Jesus asked Matthew to come and follow him (see Matthew 9:9). He invited him to be one of his 12 closest friends.

I don't think it is a coincidence that the name *Matthew* means "gift of God."[16] Because that's how Jesus saw him—as a gift. God's gift. Jesus looked past this man's reputation and saw him as he could be.

Jesus *chose* Matthew. And he turned his life around.

It almost makes me cry to think of Matthew saying yes to Jesus. His transformation is a beautiful example of what can happen in our mixed-up, selfish hearts when Jesus believes in us.

We are all disreputable characters sometimes. We do things and say things that are far from respectable more often than we would like. But we also have a God who sees the best in us. A God who invites us to walk with him and be close to him. A God who helps us be better than we ever thought we could be.

Jesus knows our character. Better than we can imagine. And he thinks of us as gifts from God.

Invite Him In

Jesus has chosen you, called you, invited you to be his disciple. It's not a position you earn by being spiritual enough, well-behaved enough, or good enough. It's an invitation to know him better and experience his unconditional love for you. Like Matthew, you are a gift of God, and he sees you as you can be. Let him turn your life around.

Prayer

Dear Jesus, I need you. I confess that I am a disreputable *character* sometimes—desperate for your mercy, your attention, your vote of confidence. Thank you that even when I act in sinful, selfish ways, you see the good—*your* good—inside me always.

COMPLETE

verb: to finish; to bring to an end; to make whole or perfect

By his Spirit he has stamped us with his eternal pledge—a
sure beginning of what he is destined to complete.
2 CORINTHIANS 1:22

Whenever I hear the word *complete*, I picture Tom Cruise standing across the room from Renée Zellweger in the movie *Jerry Maguire*. At the end of his desperate attempt to win her back, he tells her that he loves her. "You complete me," he says, wrapping up his whispered plea, and it works. So romantic (and kind of sappy) that people have quoted this movie script for over twenty years now.[17]

Complete is a feel-good word. Completing something is a big deal. Some of us complete projects, presentations, and budgets. Others complete treatment, therapy, or training. Many complete degrees, athletic endeavors, works of art. It's incredibly satisfying to reach a goal, to see something through to the end.

But completing a person? That's something only God can do. I don't mean the *Jerry Maguire* kind of completing someone. I mean the Holy Spirit kind.

Are you struggling with guilt, with secrets? Are you feeling like you can never "get right" before God? Do you worry that you are too selfish to be in a relationship with him?

The Holy Spirit kind of completing gives sinners like us a chance to be whole, to be made perfect. All we have to do is give him the guilt, the doubt, the secrets, and ask him to forgive us. He will fill our empty places and make us new.

What a gift! What a relief! He seals and keeps us. He gives us his eternal pledge that he will finish the work he began in us. We cannot possibly do this on our own.

INVITE HIM IN

Spend some time talking to Jesus, admitting your secrets and shame. Only he can make you perfect and clean before him. Ask him to do his finishing work in your heart and soul. His Spirit will seal you and complete you and make you whole.

PRAYER

Dear Jesus, thank you that your Holy Spirit seals my heart and assures me that I belong to you. Thank you that you guarantee everything you have promised. Please help me trust you every day to *complete* this work that you began in me.

RELENTLESS

adjective: showing no signs of slackening or yielding in
one's purpose; determined, persistent, tenacious

You're loyal in your steadfast love...determined in
purpose and relentless in following through.
JEREMIAH 32:18-19

Our family eagerly looks forward to watching the Olympics. As much as we love football and baseball, there is just no other sporting event that compares. The competitors, their stories, the drama, the countries coming together in spirit, the loyalty to country and sport, the challenges overcome, the unexpected medals. Millions pay attention for those few weeks of the winter or summer. It's inspiring and exciting and fun.

What really impresses me the most is the dedication of the athletes. Especially the ones who have the additional courage and tenacity to persevere through hardship, disability, loss, and failure. Some of them have given everything: years of practicing, physical and mental exhaustion, sacrificial commitment. They train for most of their lives to get to this level. Nothing has stopped them.

It's hard to imagine for most of us. We have goals, ideas, good intentions, but we get interrupted, distracted, impatient. We get off track, and back on. Back off, and back on...You know how it goes. We know we should pray, read the Bible, maybe write in a journal or memorize verses. We should go to church, get involved in a ministry, join a small group. All good and important ways to grow in our relationship with God.

But things get in our way. And we let them stop us. We are not diehards like these Olympic athletes. We get so discouraged. Luckily for us, Jesus is endlessly patient and absolutely relentless in his pursuit of us.

Even though we lose our way and don't follow through, nothing gets in Jesus's way as he reaches out to us. He made the ultimate sacrifice—living and dying to bring us to himself. He sends us messages of beauty, peace, joy, and comfort in a million creative ways. He brings new people into our lives to encourage and challenge our hearts. And he never gives up. He follows through to the very end.

INVITE HIM IN

Thank Jesus for his relentless pursuit of you. Stop for a minute and dare yourself to believe how much you truly mean to him. He gave everything he had for you. His purpose and ultimate goal was to rescue you and bring you close to him. He will not stop pursuing you, loving you, believing in you—*ever*.

PRAYER

Dear Jesus, your unfailing love saves me. Thank you for your *relentless* pursuit of me, even when I am not feeling very lovable. Your constant mercy and mighty power keep me close to you.

RESTORE

verb: to bring back; to return, to repair

GOD, your God, will restore everything you lost; he'll
have compassion on you; he'll come back and pick up the
pieces from all the places where you were scattered.
DEUTERONOMY 30:3

Totaled. Burned to the ground. Shattered. Torn.

Those are devastating descriptions. There is pain that comes from the destruction of something—a home, a car, a valuable piece of art, or a precious photograph—especially those things that cannot be replaced.

And then there is the heart-wrenching ache of losing a relationship, confidence, respect, or your place. Sometimes *we* are the ones who get lost, who feel destroyed. We wonder if we can ever get back to who we thought we were or who we were hoping to be.

We feel like we are in pieces. Not sure how to start putting ourselves together again. Maybe we are so overwhelmed that we are wondering if we even want to. It's hard to imagine what it would look like, what we would feel like to be whole again.

Whole? Put together? Renewed?

Jesus sees us like that. He designed us long before we were born. As he gently forms us throughout our lives, he has the picture in his heart of exactly how he created us to be. He is able to replace and restore the parts of us that break, that wear down, that get lost.

If we let him, he will start with a fresh breath of his Holy Spirit and begin to restore us in his perfect, careful, just-what-we-need way.

He will gently replace the broken pieces and strengthen every tired and hurting part. He will make us better, stronger, *new*.

It's not over. We're still here. He's still here too.

He can bring us back.

INVITE HIM IN

Ask Jesus for a glimpse of how he sees you. You might feel broken and scattered with parts and pieces missing, but he holds the original, beautiful design. And he is the only one who can do the deliberate, careful work of restoring you inside and out. He does it with creativity and compassion, grace and love. All you have to do is ask him. He will rebuild and restore you with all the finishing touches that make you perfectly, uniquely, completely his.

PRAYER

Dear Jesus, with all my heart and soul, I turn to you. I am in pieces, scattered in too many places, and I believe that only you can set me free. Please *restore* me to you in your compassion and bring me close.

Trouble

noun: difficulty or problems; a cause of worry or inconvenience

Disciples so often get into trouble; still, God is there every time.
Psalm 34:19

I really don't like the word *trouble.*

Nothing feels good about being in trouble, having trouble, or causing trouble.

I remember clearly the first time I got in trouble at school. I was in kindergarten. I had finally learned to climb up on top of the coat closet after watching many of my classmates accomplish this challenging and dangerous feat. As I sat there, proudly swinging my feet above the admiring faces of my friends, our teacher suddenly came around the corner and spotted me. With a volume and tone that I had never heard come out of her mouth, she demanded that I "come down right now." In one split second, my delighted heart turned ashamed and afraid. I silently vowed to stay out of trouble from that day on.

I worked awfully hard to keep my precocious and adventurous self in my teacher's good graces. I didn't want her—or anyone else, for that matter—to get angry with me. I really tried not to *get* into trouble again.

But sometimes I did.

I surely didn't want to *have* any trouble either. As I grew older and more responsible, I would diligently overplan, overpack, and overthink every situation. I felt confident that if I prepared well enough, I would be able to prevent anything from going wrong.

But, of course, it still did.

My deepest fear, though, was *being* trouble. I became quite adept at pleasing people—trying desperately to say and do what they wanted me to. I was determined not to be an inconvenience. Annoying? Difficult? Needy? I would've rather died than be any of those.

But sometimes I was.

When I talked to Jesus about this recently, I told him that I was so sorry. That I never meant to be any trouble...

His response took me by surprise and caught my heart. He lovingly, gently, and very clearly told me that I actually *am* a little bit of trouble.

I think I stopped breathing.

Immediately, he reassured me with an overwhelming sense of peace that he absolutely adores me. And this is why he came—to be with me in the middle of my mess.

It was almost as if I could see his eyes smiling at me, loving the girl he created with her adventurous, feisty spirit. Trouble and all.

INVITE HIM IN

Take a deep breath and share your troubles with Jesus. He understands the messes you get into, and he has so much compassion for you. He created you, adores you, and wants to be with you—just the way you are.

PRAYER

Dear Jesus, thank you for loving me even when I am a little bit (or a lot) of *trouble*. You know better than anyone my faults, my mistakes, and my weaknesses. Thank you that you patiently rescue me every time.

LIGHT

noun: the natural agent that makes things visible;
a source of illumination; brightness, radiance

*The prophetic Word was confirmed to us. You'll do well to keep
focusing on it. It's the one light you have in a dark time.*
2 Peter 1:19

Light is essential, captivating, beautiful. It is a gift from God. He created physical light and spiritual light to reveal, to give life, and to overcome darkness.

Light reveals. In the light, we see things as they really are. We can distinguish colors, shapes, depth, and size. We can see the path in front of us. In the light of Jesus, we see a bigger picture, we realize our need for salvation, and we discover truth. We can find our way home.

Light gives life. God created the sun to be the source of all the warmth and energy we need to survive. Every living thing depends on it. Jesus, the light of the world (John 8:12), makes us new and promises us eternal life. Through his Word and his Holy Spirit, we receive redemption, forgiveness, and the absolute assurance that we will live with him forever.

Light overcomes darkness. No matter how dark the sky, the room, or the road, the smallest flicker of light helps us see. A streetlight, a flashlight, a flame...light breaks through, taking the power of darkness away. The light of Jesus does this too. It is stronger than grief, stronger than fear, stronger than depression, stronger than shame, and stronger than pain. It is powerful enough to conquer evil and bring hope to every situation we face.

Christmas lights remind me of this. We celebrate the birth of Jesus in late December, when the days are short and the darkness is deep and cold. Driving to and from work in pitch black, the colored lights on trees and houses shine bright.

They comfort me as I remember the night my mom went home to Jesus. It was December 22. The pastor had come; his words felt new: God sent Jesus to enter our world and become Immanuel, "God with us." In the darkest time of every year, we celebrate his redeeming gift of light and love.

I had never thought of that before. In our most desperate times, when we need God the most, his light shines brightest. In that darkest night for our family, he came to us. He revealed his tender love, welcomed Mom into eternal life, and filled us with his hope that overcomes.

INVITE HIM IN

Welcome Jesus into your darkest places. Let him light them up with his love. Light a candle, look up at the stars, or put up some string lights to remind you. He has overcome the darkness. He will reveal his truth as you turn your heart, your eyes to him. He will make your life beautiful, bright, and new.

PRAYER

Dear Jesus, you shine real hope into the darkest places. Thank you for coming to me with your message of redemption and life. The *light* of your truth and love changes everything.

My Favorite Word: Jesus

proper noun: the central figure of Christianity;
the Messiah of ultimate salvation;
Immanuel ("God with us")

You...will name him Jesus—"God saves"—because
he will save his people from their sins.
MATTHEW 1:21

There are so many words to describe Jesus. He is everything to us—our Savior, redeemer, shepherd, king, friend. So many ways that he is "God with us" (see Isaiah 7:14). Isaiah 9:6 promised that "his names will be: Amazing Counselor, Strong God, Eternal Father, Prince of Wholeness."

He is our amazing counselor, holding our hearts with perfect wisdom and understanding. He knows us better than we know ourselves and deeply cares about every detail of our lives. He teaches us with grace.

He is our strong God, more powerful than any force in the universe. He will overcome all evil; he has destroyed the power of sin. He gives us victory in our battles—big and small—with his mighty strength and love.

He is our eternal Father, the only one we can completely depend on to provide for us and love us unconditionally in this life and in the life to come. He takes care of us forever and he is good.

He is our prince of wholeness, bringing completeness and calm in the roughest storms, healing broken hearts and lives, restoring relationships, and filling us with hope and peace.

Invite Him In

What words come to mind when you think of Jesus? Ask him to show you more and more of who he is and what he wants to do in your heart, your life. Thank him for being everything you need today and the rest of your life.

Prayer

Dear *Jesus*, thank you that you are Immanuel, "God with us." You bring salvation and freedom to everyone who calls on you. Thank you for the power, the love, the grace, and the joy that fills my heart when I say your precious name. Amen.

Notes

Devotions using definitions taken or adapted from *Merriam-Webster.com*, 2018, https://www.merriam-webster.com (accessed July 1, 2016–May 8, 2018): *Displace, Unfolding, Outcome, Rest, Run, Wreck, News, Path, Lifeline, Hide, True, Courage, Shoulders, Indispensable, Anyway, Stick, Wait, Why, Keep, Stay, Adventure, Sure, Yet, Deserve, Best, Flow, Unforced, Be, Steep, Receive, Set, Multiply, Extravagant, Splash, Energy, Dimensions, Invite, Yes, Untying, Tend, Name, Joy, Help, Forget, See, Wild, More, Colors, Container, Detail, Mystery, Rescue, Rules, Misfit, Pieces, Finish, Characters, Complete, Relentless*

Devotions using definitions taken or adapted from *Oxford American Writer's Thesaurus* Copyright © 2012, 2016 by Oxford University Press, Inc. All rights reserved: *Rest, News, Rooted, Headlong, Brave, Fresh, Enough, Deserve, Unforced, Open, Splash*

Devotions using definitions taken or adapted from *New Oxford American Dictionary* Copyright © 2010, 2017 by Oxford University Press, Inc. All rights reserved: *Roomy, Hold, Naked, Breakfast, Clearly, Sand, Wear, Container, Different, Restore, Trouble*

Devotions using definitions taken from both the *New Oxford American Dictionary* and the *Oxford American Writer's Thesaurus: Instead, Prepared, Strength, Halfway, Found (adapted from Find), Fierce, Real, Perfect, Embrace, Shower, Wonder, Part, Useless, Together, Light*

---

1. Henri Nouwen, *The Inner Voice of Love* (New York: Doubleday, 1996), 113.

2. Stephen Ira, *Velcro Brand Fasteners and NASA*, Hook and Loop, https://hookandloop.com/blog/velcro-brand-fasteners-nasa (January 17, 2014).

3. "Advent." *Merriam-Webster.com*. Merriam-Webster, n.d. Web. 6 May 2018.

4. Oswald Chambers, *My Utmost for His Highest* (New York: Dodd, Mead and Company, 1935), April 29 reading.

5. "Arrange." https://en.oxforddictionaries.com. *New Oxford American Dictionary*, 2018.

6. "Wonder Woman Destroys Ares 'Goodbye Brother'," *Wonder Woman*, directed by Patty Jenkins (Burbank, CA: Warner Brothers, 2017), DVD. https://youtube/9MHHV-uyYjM May 6, 2018.

7. https://www.nhlbi.nih.gov/health-topics/raynauds May 6, 2018.

8. "Amazing Grace," John Newton, 1779, public domain.

9. https://en.wikipedia.org/wiki/Antilia_(building).

10. *Susie*, SheKnows, http://www.sheknows.com/baby-names/name/susie (May 6, 2018).

11. http://psalm139journey.blogspot.com/2010/05/day-22-counting-grains-of-sand.html (October 20, 2017).

12. https://askdruniverse.wsu.edu/2016/06/30/smallest-insect-earth/.

13. *Crayons*, Crayola, http://shop.crayola.com/color-and-draw/crayons (May 7, 2018).

14. http://mentalfloss.com/article/82177/scientists-accidentally-discover-new-shade-blue (May 7, 2018).

15. https://en.wikipedia.org/wiki/Kintsugi (May 8, 2018).

16. https://www.behindthename.com/name/matthew (May 8, 2018).

17. "Scene #60," *Jerry Maguire*, directed by Cameron Crowe (Culver City, CA: Sony Pictures Home Entertainment, 1996), DVD.